The Team Room

Bill Raskin

ISBN: 978-1-7329944-6-1

Cover design credit: Rachel Lawston at Lawston Design
Formatting: Polgarus Studio

Inside photo credit:
https://unsplash.com/photos/UDDULE_eIBY. Presented by
Sidekix Media on Unsplash

Dedicated to all those Americans - past, present, and future - who serve in the apprenticeship of excellence that is the US Special Operations community.

Contents

CHARACTERS

DAI-UY**

The Captain.
(**Pronounced "die-wee." The Vietnamese word for "captain." See Glossary at end for an expanded list of military terms, pronunciations, and definitions.)

TOP

The Team Sergeant. A veteran of Mogadishu and Panama.

JOSE

Intel Sergeant and acting Senior Weapons Sergeant.

WES

Junior Weapons Sergeant.

BILLY

Senior Engineer.

TODD

Junior Engineer.

DOC HOLLINS

Senior Medic, though he only arrived to the team within the past eighteen months.

DALE

Junior Commo.

THE CADET	An ROTC cadet who arrived for a two-week ride-along program.

NEWS PERSONALITIES - IN ORDER OF APPEARANCE

DAVID STANSFIELD	National news anchor, based in New York, for the World Broadcasting Service (WBS) television network.
JULIAN BURKE	WBS field reporter.
SALLY PUTNAM	WBS field reporter.
ELLIOT JACKSON	WBS Washington Bureau Chief.

SETTING

The team room for Operational Detachment - Alpha 824
(ODA 824, also known as an A Team), based at Camp
Diamond, West Virginia.

TIME

Early morning, immediately after morning physical
training, or PT.

ACT I

Opens in the team room   Morning of 9/10/2001

ACT II

Opens in the team room   Morning of 9/11/2001

Upstage

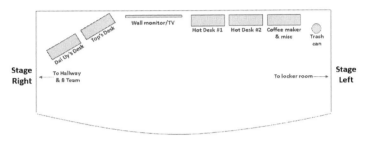

Stage Right

Stage Left

Wall monitor/TV

Hot Desk #1   Hot Desk #2   Coffee maker & misc   Trash can

Dai Uy's Desk   Top's Desk

To Hallway & B Team

To locker room

Audience

ACT [1]
SCENE [1]

(The scene opens in the team
room for Special Forces ODA
824, immediately after
morning physical training, or
"PT." The wall monitor shows
0740 hours on 9/10/2001.)

CADET
(Enters from stage right, dressed in PT gear
and drenched in sweat. Walks/stumbles across
the stage to the trash can, where he collapses
on all fours and begins to vomit.)

DOC HOLLINS
(Enters from stage right. He walks over to
stand beside the Cadet.)

CADET
Doc, I'll never survive two weeks of this!
(Vomits again.)

DOC HOLLINS
Don't panic. You'll be OK. You just showed up for Monster
Mondays is all.

1

CADET

Monster Mondays?

DOC HOLLINS

Top runs his hardest workout of the week right up front. It's
his way of keeping everyone in line. A reminder for the
young single guys, not to get too crazy over the weekend.

CADET

(Finished vomiting. Pushes himself off the
trash can and remains sitting on the ground.
Weary and breathing heavily, he looks up at
Doc. He starts to say something, but then
sinks into a slightly deeper, exhausted state.)

DOC HOLLINS

(Empathetic smile)
C'mon, I'm putting some saline in you.

CADET

Huh?

DOC HOLLINS

An IV bag. I'm giving you an IV. It will get you back on
your feet.
(Pause)
Then I'll show you where the locker rooms are. Get cleaned
up and head back here. And don't worry. (Beat.) Monster
Mondays have beat down far better men than you.

(Offers the Cadet a hand and pulls him to his feet.)

CADET

(Looks confused at how to take that statement.)

(Doc and the Cadet exit stage left.)

(Pause of several seconds.)

(Jose and Billy enter from stage right, also in sweaty PT gear.)

BILLY

Who's the kid at PT? The one talking to Top and Doc?

JOSE

He's one of those ROTC cadets. Come to do a ride-along with the team.

BILLY

Dufus, don't be a dufus! They come to post in the sum-mer-time. This is Sep-tem-ber. (Beat.) And besides, I never saw one hang with an A Team before.

JOSE

Hey, dufus! He's from one of those fancy Ivy League schools. I guess they go to school when they want. And when they don't, they don't. (Beat.) I don't know, ask Top.

TOP

(Enters from stage right.)

Ask Top what?

(He's a little grumpy. Walks past them, to the coffee maker, and begins to brew a pot.)

BILLY

Top, what's up with that Cadet?

TOP

(Holding an empty coffee mug, staring at the coffee maker and waiting for it to brew.)

Last I saw, Doc was draggin' him off for an emergency PT-ectomy.

BILLY

No, I mean, why is he here now, in the fall? And why with us?

TOP

(Looks from the coffee maker to Billy.)

Jesus, Billy! You're worse than my kids. I don't know. Ask the Cadet.

(To Jose.)

You two are running the range tomorrow. We tracking?

JOSE

Roger, Top. We'll have two DMVs for maneuver, and four thousand rounds - all calibers. We're set.

TOP

Not four thousand rounds, sixteen.

JOSE

Sixteen, what the hell?

TOP

End of the fiscal year is what the hell. The B Team dumped the rest of their excess on us.

BILLY
(Exasperated.)
C'mon, Top! The B Team can't manage *their* ammo account, and now that's our problem?

TOP

You two let me get some coffee in peace! Work call's at zero-nine-thirty. Jose, lay on whatever extra DMVs and guns you need, and tell the B Team they *will* cough 'em up. So we can bail their feet from the fire.
(Looks at Billy.)

Billy, draw up a new training plan for the range, and tell me how many extra bodies you need to shoot all them rounds. I'll hit the other teams and grab hostages to pull triggers.

JOSE

Roger that, Top.

BILLY
(To Jose.)
C'mon, let's clean up and then figure out this goat rodeo.
(Jose and Billy exit stage left.)

(Fade.)

ACT [1]
SCENE [2]

(The scene opens on the ODA
824 team room. The wall
monitor clock scrolls forward
to 0830 hours on 9/10/2001.)

(The Cadet enters from stage left, now in
uniform, and unknowingly sits at Top's desk,
facing the audience. He still looks weary from
PT.)

DALE
(Enters from stage right. A boisterous
personality.)

Whoa there, partner! That's Top's desk. You *don't* want to
get caught sitting *there.*

(The Cadet looks to Dai Uy's desk, indicating
he plans to shift to that desk.)

DALE
No, no, no. That's Dai Uy's! Here, man.

(He points to the two hot desks.)

Those are the hot desks.

(The Cadet moves over to hot desk #2 and
sits down.)

DALE

I'm Dale.

(Offers a hand, smiling.)

CADET

Hi, I'm…

DALE

You're the Cadet, I know. Billy told me. Say, how come you're not here in summer?

CADET

I'm on the quarter system.

DALE

Ahhh, yes, the quarter system. Well, that explains it all.

CADET

(Nods in agreement.)

DALE

What the hell is the quarter system? Jeez! You officers and future officers. Y'all have a world all your own. And then you expect the rest of us to just understand it.

CADET

Oh, sorry! At Dartmouth. We go to school year-round, on academic quarters. You pick which one you take off for break. I took fall quarter off, and my ROTC detachment let me come down here on ride-along.

                    DALE

And you asked to shadow a Special Forces team? That took guts.

                    CADET
               (Looking sheepish.)
Well, not exactly.

                    DALE
          (Amused, awaits an explanation.)

                    CADET

I...I asked for *Camp Diamond*, yes, but not Special Forces specifically. I asked for this post because of this girl I met at a concert. She goes to State, just down the road. I didn't even know there was a Special Forces unit here.

                    DALE
            (Laughs uproariously.)
Well, if you survive until Friday, maybe you can lick your wounds and go see Miss State U!

                    CADET

At least I got past Monster Mondays.

DALE

Yeah, but didn't they tell you about Freaky Fridays? Monster
Mondays is *nuthin'*.

CADET

(Horrified.)

What?

DALE

(Laughs.)

I'm just joshin'! There's no Freaky Fridays. You'll be OK.
(Slaps the Cadet on the shoulder.)

Say, you on email yet? I'm the Junior Commo guy. It's my
job to get you hooked up.

CADET

(Looks at the laptop on the desk.)

No, I'm not on email.

DALE

(Points to the laptop.)

Here, let me drive, we'll set up a temp account.

(Dale and the Cadet swap places at hot desk
#2.)

DALE

(Working on the computer.)

OK, we'll call your account "Cadet User 1." I'll send an email on the team distro, so they'll all have it.

CADET

Hey, thanks!
          (Pause)
I have to run out to my car. The B Team needs a copy of my orders. You need anything else from me, for the temp account?

DALE

          (Keeps working, doesn't look up from the
          computer.)
Nope, got you all hooked up.

CADET

Thanks again.
          (Exits stage right.)

DALE

          (Still working on the computer, a new
          thought pops into his head. He looks off to
          stage right and realizes the Cadet is gone and
          he's alone. He thinks for a moment. Then he
          wags his head in merriment and starts to talk
          out loud as he types.)
Subject: You'd better watch out
          (Pauses, then talks aloud as he types in the
          email main body.)

You guys might be laughing at getting the better of me in PT today. But it was just the high humidity is all. I'm not used to the swamp atmosphere down here. But you'd better treat me good. I'm still growing, and I'll get stronger. From the looks of it, I'll get stronger than all of you. And one day, I'll probably come back here and command this team.

> (Hits the enter button with a dramatic flair. Next, he grabs a newspaper that's sitting by the coffee maker on the adjacent table. He turns around to face the audience and begins to read it silently.)

WES

> (Enters in PT gear from stage right. Gets coffee and sits down at hot desk #1. He logs on. He has a serious look on his face.)

DALE

Wes, my man. You were smokin' it at PT today.

WES

I don't know about that. My mile splits are five-forty, but I oughta be breaking five-thirties for the work I'm putting in. That creatine doesn't seem to be doing a damn thing.

> (Opens his email account.)

DALE

> (Keeps reading the paper. He gives a furtive glance over to Wes.)

WES

(Angry.)

What the hell!

DALE

(Puts the paper down and looks over at Wes.)

What's up?

WES

Did you put that cadet on email?

DALE

Yeah, man. He's gonna be here for two weeks.

WES

Well, he's got some serious trouble coming his way. Look at
what he wrote!

DALE

(Looks over at the laptop, reads, and then
whistles.)

Man, yeah. Someone should probably put him in his place.

WES

(Types loudly, hits send, and then logs out.
Says angrily.)

I'm going to clean up. That little punk.

(Exits stage left.)

DALE
(Looks up from his paper to make sure he's
alone. Then, with a smirk on his face, turns
around to the laptop at his desk. He reads out
loud Wes's email response.)

Cadet, I don't know who the hell you think you are. But you
and I are going to have a *talk*.

(Pauses, then Dale talks to himself.)

OK, Mr. Wes! How do we reply? Hmmmm.

(He wags his head in merriment again, while
rapidly typing on the keyboard.)

(After hitting send and logging off, Dale exits
stage left.)

(Fade.)

ACT [1]
SCENE [3]

> (The scene opens on the ODA
> 824 team room. The wall
> monitor clock scrolls forward
> to 0855 hours on 9/10/2001.)

(Jose and Billy enter from stage left, in
uniform. The Cadet enters from stage right.)

CADET

Hi, I'm...

BILLY

We know. You're the Cadet. How are you doing? Doc
Hollins hook you up?

> (Jose and Billy each grab a cup
> of coffee and then take seats at
> hot desks #1 and #2.)

CADET

Yeah, he sure did! I feel like a new person after that IV.

BILLY

Well, he's still new, but he's the best medic in the battalion.
He's also the best sniper in the battalion - won the last two
shoot offs. I guess you could say, Doc personifies the "no

better friend, no worse enemy" theory of international relations.

CADET

(Confused.)

But how can a medic be a sniper? I thought they're not allowed?

JOSE

Man, what do they teach you in ROTC? Didn't you study up on us before asking for a ride-along?

CADET

(Says uncomfortably.)

Well, I wasn't sure - exactly - where I would go.

BILLY

Dude, on a Special Forces A Team, *everybody* fights.

JOSE

And everybody has specialty skills, too.

(Jose and Billy lean forward
and grow more focused,
slightly more intense, as they
provide the Cadet with a
rapid-fire tutorial.)

BILLY

It's more than that. Our specialty is unconventional warfare.
Going in behind the lines and leading partisan groups. Just
like the OSS did in Yugoslavia in World War II, against the
Germans.

JOSE

That makes us combat multipliers.

BILLY

Combat mul-ti-pli-ers. Get it?

CADET

Um, not really?

BILLY

Multipliers, man! It means when you let our team on the
ground, you're not just dealing with us. With our little team.
            (Pause.)
You're dealing with *hundreds* of locals that we train,
organize, and lead. You're dealing with the *resistance network*
we're able to build. The local leaders we're going to build
relationships with. The *movements* we're capable of shaping.
All in the name of US national security and foreign policy.

CADET

And you do all that with just twelve of you?

JOSE

Hah, twelve on paper. There's never any twelve.
> (Pause.)

Life gets in the way, my friend. Right now, we've got nine on paper. But our Senior Commo, Jim, is off at ANCOC. (Pronounced "ay-nock".) So we'll roll to the field tomorrow with eight. A new Special Forces course, the "Q-Course," graduates in December. *Maybe* we'll get some plus-ups from that.

BILLY

It's like this. On paper, we're a twelve-man A Team. That starts with our four primary skills: weapons, medical, engineering, and commo. Each of those has a senior and a junior. That's eight team members. I'm Senior Engineer.
> (Points to Jose.)

And my far less handsome friend here, he graduated up from Weapons NCO to be our Intel Sergeant. But we're short a weapons man. So Top dual-hats Jose as our Senior Weapons. Anyway, the Intel Sergeant is the ninth man on the team.

JOSE

Then there's big-daddy-team-daddy. Our team sergeant. For us, that's Top, in the tenth authorized position.

CADET

Why is he called Top?

BILLY

Top, for top sergeant. It's an old Army term. And believe me, Top has old Army in his DNA.

(Pause.)

And then you got two officers, for slots eleven and twelve. A warrant officer as the Deputy, and a captain as the team commander.

JOSE

Only there's almost never both officers. We get maybe one or the other. So for us, we've got Dai Uy.

CADET

Dai Uy?

JOSE

Dai Uy is Vietnamese for "captain." From back in the war. When Top was a young man, his first team had a lot of Vietnam vets on it. Top likes the nickname.

BILLY

And as you'll see around here, what Top likes, goes.

CADET

Yeah, I caught that about Monster Mondays, too!

JOSE

(Hearty laugh.)

Yes, Sir. You don't show up ready for Monster Mondays, and Top's gonna give you the what-for.

CADET

So, are you saying Top's really in charge? He's the one calling all the shots?

BILLY

No, dude. Dai Uy *is* the Dai Uy. (Beat.) The Captain *is* the Captain.

> (Looks to the Cadet, seeking affirmation that he understands.)

CADET

(Clearly, he doesn't understand.)

JOSE

It's like this. Top *runs* the team. But the Captain, he *commands* it. An ODA is a complex animal. We might have a dicey unilateral mission, where it's just our team but we're really threading the needle. Or we might be pushing hundreds of indigenous fighters out at the end of the earth. Either way, a good captain and team sergeant, like our Dai Uy and Top, they share the load.

CADET

Like *mom* and *dad?*

JOSE

Exactly! Top's the team daddy. You get it. And then, just like any family, mom gets the final word.

BILLY

But, if Dai Uy's about to really screw up, Top will save him from himself. Officers, they get schoolhouse schooling. But Top, he's got a PhD from the *street*.
(Looking at Jose and nudging him.)
Tell him about Canada. Perfect example of *both* cases.

JOSE
(Laughs.)
Yes, that's a good example. That was last year, when Dai Uy first came to the team. He put together a long-range movement exercise. Over a hundred and thirty klicks in all, through mountains that were just *brutal*.

BILLY

Up in the Canadian Rockies.

JOSE

My hat's off to Dai Uy. All that coordination with the Canucks…

BILLY

Huuuuge red tape!

JOSE

Dai Uy, he's quiet but persistent. He plowed through all that paperwork. Went up and met with their park rangers, our consulate, their customs, all of it.

(Pause.)

He spent weeks finalizing the mission, back here at Camp Diamond. Finally, it came time for infil.

BILLY

Military free fall. Twenty-thousand-foot night jump, O2, into the absolute middle of nowhere. It was so remote, we had to cache our chutes at the start point. Then we flew back in by helicopter, at the end, to retrieve 'em.

JOSE

Infil, it was a total mess. When we were on the aircraft ramp, right as Top gave the "follow me" for us to jump, we hit an ungodly air pocket.

BILLY

Knocked the hell out of us. Bounced us off the roof of the aircraft and then right off the ramp. I couldn't see straight for half a day.

JOSE

Dai Uy, he caught it the worst. It knocked him clean unconscious. (Beat.) We all thought he was dead. That cat tumbled all the way down to 2,500 feet AGL, above-ground-level. None of us could catch him. Top chased him all the way down until wave off.

CADET

(Captivated.)
Oh my gosh! What happened?

BILLY

The AOD saved his ass.

CADET

AOD?

JOSE

His automatic opening device. It's set to the barometric pressure of your pull altitude, and deploys the main canopy if you're incapacitated. There's still a hundred ways it can go wrong, when you're tumbling like that. But Dai Uy got lucky. It fired just fine. Under canopy, Dai Uy woke up just in time to go to half brakes and not snap his neck.

BILLY

Here's what you got to understand. That air pocket so beat us to hell and scattered us, it was dawn before we all limped in to our linkup point. We circled up in a patrol base and took stock.

(Laughs hard.)
And Dai Uy, man. The g-force, from how bad he'd been spinning, it burst *all* the capillaries in his eyes. Solid red! He

looked like a zombie. Now, old Dai Uy, he's a hard charger. He wanted just to get us up and moving. Top and Jose pushed *hard* that we should take a few hours and rest up. We needed to lick our wounds.

JOSE

We really made the case, how bad we were beaten up, and needed to recoup.

CADET

What happened then?

BILLY

Dai Uy looked at us and announced, "OK, I've got an alternate plan." And we start smiling like it's Christmas. Our reprieve! (Beat.) And then Dai Uy says, "We're gonna suck it up, and drive on."

JOSE
(Now it's his turn to laugh.)
Nobody said a thing. You could hear the despair. And then Top just nodded his head. It was a command decision.
(Pause.)
Dai Uy knew the score. We needed every minute of every day. Or else we'd never make the rendezvous time at the end. You can see where he was coming from. I mean, his first team deployment. He moved heaven and earth to coordinate that thing. It would have been egg on *all* our faces, if we didn't make that rendezvous.

CADET

(Nods silently.)

BILLY

But there's other times, a good captain's gonna have to know when to give. Because a good team sergeant might just save his ass.

JOSE

Like with the bear.

BILLY

(Nods.)
Like with the bear.

CADET

What was "the bear"?

BILLY

It was on that same training movement, in Canada. Two days after infil.

JOSE

There was a couple issues for us, doing that movement. It was all on Canadian national park land. They were very accommodating to us. But on two rules, they would not budge. One - no ammo.

BILLY

Not a big deal, we figured. Down here, we go to the field all the time with no ammo.

JOSE

And issue number two for the Canucks - pack out *all* trash. MREs especially.

BILLY

Again, no big deal. We always do that. But like, they made the point they'd *inspect* us, to *make sure* we packed out everything. They really follow the whole "leave no trace" principle. Nastygram to the State Department and all, if you blow it off.

JOSE

By the end of the second day on that movement, we were finally getting into a groove. It was almost dusk. We were moving into higher altitude. We needed a few hours' rest. So we set up a patrol base in the last bit of tree cover. Some real nice firs.

BILLY

Just like always, Top set up the perimeter. He went around and assigned each of us our positions and sectors of fire.

JOSE

Dai Uy was at his usual spot in the center of the circle. He was preparing our daily SATCOM report back to headquarters. But then he went over and told Top how there were bear tracks around. *Big* bear tracks.

BILLY

Now Top, he's country bred through and through. You could drop him in the woods with nothing but a pocket knife, and a month later he'd walk out fat and happy.

JOSE

Dai Uy, he's a great officer. But he's a city fella. Top kept blowing him off. Kept moving around the perimeter and setting up sectors.

BILLY

And finally, about the time Top finished, Dai Uy said for like the third time, "Top, really, you gotta come check out these bear tracks. "

JOSE

Top sort of rolled his eyes. He walked over with Dai Uy, just to humor him.

BILLY

(Belly laughs.)

And Top, he took one look at those footprints, and he says, "Oh my God! Those are bear tracks alright. They're the biggest bear tracks I ever saw!"

JOSE

It's not just that they were grizzly tracks. We've seen grizzly. Top's seen more grizzly than you can shake a stick at. But these footprints, they were like *alien big*.

(Holds his hands up, two feet apart.)

BILLY

Twenty-four inches for sure. World record big!

CADET

(Can't contain his excitement.)

Tell me! What happened next?

BILLY

Wes and Todd went to hang our bag, with all our MREs, MRE trash and stuff, just like we'd been doin' every patrol base. Hundred-fifty meters outside our perimeter. Then we went into security plan, and rotated catching z's.

(Pause.)

Later, after dark, we heard this just terrible, just awful thrashing over where we hung the bag. Finally, the noise stopped. It stayed quiet as a church after that. Then, at zero-two-hundred, we started packing up to move.

JOSE

Wes and Todd, they went over to pull down the food bag. And then they shouted for the whole team to come over. (Beat.) They showed us with a red lens.

BILLY

They'd hung that bag in a branch, thirty feet off the ground.
And there wasn't a *single* branch left on that tree up to the
twenty-foot mark. All these good-sized branches were just
piled on the ground.

> (With his hands forms a circle eight inches in
> diameter.)

JOSE

That beast darn near took down the whole tree! It clawed
more than halfway through the trunk.

BILLY

We packed ASAP and got out of there by zero-two-thirty.
Started moving upslope, through the next piece of mountain
range.

JOSE

And the rest of the night, damned if we can't *hear* that bear.
It followed us! It could smell that MRE trash.

> (Pause.)

It got to be dawn. By then we were almost above tree line.
We were in all these juniper bushes that go just a little over
your head.

> (Holds his hand up to indicate the height.)

BILLY

And behind us, we start seeing all the Juniper bushes swaying. Not fifty meters away. Then we caught glimpses of the top of its head. Scary big!

JOSE

It was getting serious. (Beat.) So Top, he called us all into a big clump. To make us look like one big animal. We all shouted and clapped, hoping to make noise and finally send it away. And that bear, it just kept inching its way forward. Forty-five meters. Forty meters. It must have been big fool hungry. (Beat.) It didn't charge us. It just kept closing in…closing in.

CADET

Tell me! What happened?

JOSE

Top finally barks out, "Get every bit of MRE trash you all got, and leave it right here on the ground! Right here in one big pile. Then we're gonna un-ass this place."

BILLY

And with all that going on, Dai Uy's thinking about those park rangers he's got to answer to, and he says, "Top, we can't leave the trash! We'll get in huge trouble!"

(Nudges Jose.)

JOSE

And Top turns right back on Dai Uy and says, "Sir, you can't
get in no more trouble than get ate by a bear!"

(Jose and Billy both cackle for several
moments.)

CADET

Did Dai Uy give the order?

BILLY

(Laughs.)
Didn't have to. Soon as Top said that, the rest of us had our
trash on the ground. We un-assed that place, pronto. (Beat.)
And that's the last we ever heard from that bear.

JOSE

So, you see, my future officer, the moral of the Canada story?
When in charge, *take charge*. But, if you're about to be eaten
by the bear, then listen to your team daddy!
(Top walks in from stage right. He looks at
Jose and Billy.)

TOP

Don't you two have a range to plan? The Army's not paying
for you to jaw jack.

BILLY

We're heading out now, Top.

TOP

Jose. That Mark-19, last time we had it out there.
(Raises an eyebrow.)

JOSE

(Sighs, frustrated.)
Roger. It was hanging up every fifth or sixth round - bad feed slide assembly. Battalion had a spare on bench stock. Wes and I already swapped it out and test fired it on C Company's range last week.

TOP

Good job. Tomorrow we'll hear it singin' smooth as Shania Twain.

JOSE

(Nods.)
Roger that.

BILLY

(To the Cadet.)
C'mon, help us in the arms room. You'll learn something.

(Jose, Billy, and the Cadet walk toward stage right.)

BILLY

(Hums Shania Twain. Then to Jose, he sings in tune to one of her songs.)

That don't impress me much!

JOSE

Shut up.

(They all three exit.)

TOP

(Sits down at the laptop on his desk and logs on.)

WES

(Enters from stage left, gets coffee and sits at hot desk #2.)

Hey, Top.

(He logs onto the laptop.)

TOP

(Still working and not looking up.)

Wes.

(They each work in silence.)

WES

(Looking at an email he has opened.)
Oh God damn it! I am going to beat down that little punk!

TOP

(Still looking at his own screen.)

Who?

WES

That cadet. (Beat.) Top, look at what he wrote. That God-
damn little punk! I am going to beat him down like a dog.
Listen to this!

(Reads from the screen.)

"Wes, you old fat back. If you think you can handle what
I've got for you, then just slink your ass out to the combatives
pit. And when I'm done with you, I'm going to do you a
favor. I'm going to take you down to the meat department
at Food Lion, and buy you some back bone."

(Pause)

That little punk, I am going to *beat him down*!

TOP

(Looks over his shoulder at Wes,
incredulous.)

What?

(Walks over to where Wes is working. Reads
over his shoulder.)

Show me that whole thread.

(Reads as Wes scrolls the thread for him. He
looks skeptical and then transitions to
laughter.)

Oh, Mr. Wes. I don't think it was our young cadet wrote
that.

WES

What are you talking about? It's straight from his email!

TOP

Wes, who does that have the smell of?
(Raises an eyebrow.)

WES

(Thinks for a moment.)

Dale!

(Stands up, looking at Top.)

Well, I don't care who it is. But someone is taking a beat-down!

TOP

(Continues to silently chuckle and shake his
head as he walks back to his desk. He sits and
waves one hand up over his shoulder, as if
washing away the episode.)

(Fade.)

ACT [1]
SCENE [4]

(The scene opens on the ODA
824 team room. The wall
monitor clock scrolls forward
to 0925 hours on 9/10/2001.)

(Doc and the Cadet walk in from stage right.
The Cadet is disheveled and walks unsteadily.
Doc holds him by the right elbow and guides
him over to sit at hot desk #2.)

CADET

(Alarmed.)
What the HELL was that?

DOC HOLLINS

(Irritated.)
That is what we call around here "Wild Wild Wes." (Beat)
Sometimes he gets spun up.

CADET

I can tell!

DOC HOLLINS

I'm glad I walked through the arms room when I did.
(Puzzled look on his face.)

The question is, why was he spun up on *you?*

CADET

I have no idea!

DOC HOLLINS

Well, he might be the hardest man on the team. Don't tell him I said that. And you just survived a run-in with him. So that's something.
            (Pause.)
Don't worry. He wouldn't have blown up that bad, except I stepped in.

CADET

Why would he be mad at you?

DOC HOLLINS

We're not exactly on each other's Christmas card list.

CADET

(Exhales loudly and shakes his head.)

WES

(Enters from stage right, angry. Points at Doc.)
Damn it, Doc! You don't tell me what to do!

DOC HOLLINS

(Speaks in control, but angry.)

Wes, this is like last time. (Beat) *You* don't get in my face. Now get out of here and get your shit together.

WES

(Takes a step closer, points again.)

I don't work for you!

DOC HOLLINS

(Takes a step closer as well. Coldness in his voice.)

It's comin', Wes. You know our day's comin'.

WES

Doc, I may not be the pretty-boy teacher's pet. But trust me, when that day does come, you're going to regret it.

(Wes and Doc stare silently at each other for several beats. From where the Cadet is seated, he watches anxiously and in silence.)

WES

(Slowly turns and exits stage right, angry.)

DOC HOLLINS

(Stands for a couple beats, watching Wes depart. Then he exits stage left.)

CADET

(Sits for a few moments and takes in the exchange he just witnessed. Then he turns

and logs on to the laptop at his desk. He reads
through emails on his temporary account.)

Oh. No. (Beat.) Fat back!

(Pause.)

Meat department at Food Lion?

(Pause of several seconds as the Cadet
continues to take in the shock.)

DALE

(Enters from stage right. Somewhat
embarrassed at realizing the Cadet is reading
through the emails Dale sent in the Cadet's
name.)

How are you, man? I heard about the arms room fracas.

CADET

Dale! That was you. You sent those emails! Why did you do
that?

DALE

I'm sorry, man. Was just having a little fun was all. I should
have thought it through more. Sometimes Wes cooks off like
that.

(Pause.)

It damn sure doesn't help that Wes and Doc got into it again.
Top is gonna be all over my ass if he finds out. Don't say
anything about them fighting just now, OK?

CADET

OK.

DALE

Thanks, I'll make it up to you.

CADET

(Now curious.)

Why does Wes hate Doc?

DALE

Hmm.

(He thinks on it.)

It's not hate, really.

(Pause.)

Wes *resents* Doc. Doc takes up his space. Not on purpose.
Doc's just one of those supremely talented guys, even for an
A Team. And without even thinking about it, he can just
sort of take up people's space.

CADET

But *you're* not mad at Doc.

DALE

It's different for me. Wes doesn't want to wait for anything.
He's a guy in a hurry. Wants to do it all. But Doc can do it
all *just a little bit better*. So then Wes gets resentful.
Threatened, almost. And when it gets to be too much, he
gets in Doc's face.

CADET

(Thinks silently for a moment.)
But Doc said Wes might be the hardest man on the team.

DALE

Oh, he is! By far. Wes could take down any *two* men on this
team.

CADET

Then wouldn't that be enough? For Wes not to feel
threatened?

DALE

Look, Doc and Wes, they're the two newest on the team.
Doc got here eighteen months ago. And Wes about six
months after that.
(Pause.)
And Doc, he had a lot of advantages that let him just hit the
ground running. Fast.

CADET

Such as?

DALE

Well, first of all, he's older. Doc went to college for pre-med.
He was going to medical school. Married, had a kid already.
He had it all figured out.

41

CADET

What happened?

DALE

Doc's wife, Natalie.
>(Pause.)

Jeez, man. I've caused enough trouble for one day. Let me respect the man's privacy a little bit. Short story is - she came down with a lifetime health condition.
>(Pause.)

Doc, he ran the numbers. No way they could afford the health care *and* pay for all the schooling it takes to be a doctor.

CADET

So he joined the Army?

DALE

Yeah, he joined the Infantry. Served at Fort Hood. And Natalie stabilized more. (Beat.) Enough. (Beat.) They talked. And she said, since he missed out going to med school, what did he want to do in the Army? Really *do?* And Doc, by then he'd met some Special Forces guys. And he said he wanted to go SF. And Natalie, she said OK.

CADET

But how does that threaten Wes?

DALE

It's just the whole *package*, of how Doc takes up space. Most teams, like us, don't have but one medic on the books. So Doc walks in, and right away that makes him a *senior*, not a junior. Callin' some shots right away. Wes comes along as a weapons sergeant. And Jose has technically stepped up to be our Intel Sergeant. But Top is an old-school weapons man himself. He doesn't trust his guns to just anyone. So Top told Jose he's still Senior Weapons *and* our Intel NCO. Now Wes, he takes it all like one big "Wait in line, dude" kind of insult.

CADET

(Nods.)

DALE

And Doc's one of these guys just freaky good, at everything he does. He's got surgeon's hands, right? He can work his way around most of our weapons better than either Wes *or* Jose.

(Pause.)

Jose, he's a *good* weapons man, and he knows it. He's got confidence in his experience. Doc being so good, it rolls off his back. But Wes, it bothers him to no end.

CADET

Like when Doc won the sniper competition?

DALE

Oh, hell yes! Think about it. Our brand-new medic shows up and wins, straight away. He wins again this year. Salt in the wound, man. 'Cause when Doc won this year, guess who'd also arrived by then and came in *second place?*

CADET

Wes?

DALE

Yessir. Wes was the honor grad of his Q Course, just six months behind Doc. Wes got honor grad at Ranger School, too - when he was in the 11th Airborne. Hell, the 11th Airborne made him a squad leader even, as a brand-new E-5.

(Pause.)

And Wes is a beast. His favorite thing is to put on body armor during PT and then go run down entire *teams* out on their training runs. The man's used to bein' lead stud at *everything* he's done.

CADET

Until he gets here.

DALE

Ex-actly. There's *fifty-four* teams in this Group, spread across three *Battalions.* Wes goes to any other ODA, and he's the standout stud on the team. He goes to a team in another battalion and he's the standout new guy in the *Battalion.* But he lost the lottery. He landed here, and he's fightin' for his oxygen. That's why the rest of us call Wes and Doc the Clash of the Titans.

CADET

(Nods.)

Got it.

DALE

Anyway, man. Like I said, sorry 'bout messing with you. You good?

CADET

I'm good.

DALE

OK, let me get in the arms room and help out. I need to earn up some karma, for when Top learns about the ruckus I caused.

CADET

Need help?

DALE

Nah. Hang in here and let the dust settle.

(Smiles.)

See ya.

(Exits stage right.)

CADET

(Turns to the laptop on hot desk #2 and
continues reading.)

TODD

(Enters from stage right, still in sweaty PT
gear. Approaches the Cadet.)

Hey, I'm Todd.

CADET

(Stands and they shake hands.)

Hi, I'm…

TODD

You're the Cadet. We heard. You're here two weeks?

CADET

Yes, that's right.

(The Cadet sits back down at hot desk #2.)

Why are you still in PT gear? Didn't work call start already?

TODD

(Sits at hot desk #1 and logs on.)

Yeah. I was out in the parking lot, finishing some phone
calls.

(Keeps working on the computer.)

CADET

What do you do on the team?

TODD

I'm the Junior Engineer.
                    (Continues scrolling through screens.)

CADET

That's demolitions, right?

TODD
                    (Looking at the Cadet.)
Uh, yeah. Demolitions is part of it. I can blow up anything.
                    (Pause.)
But, you know, as team engineers, we do a whole lot more.

CADET

Like what?

TODD

Well, we do construction, too.

CADET

Like buildings?

TODD

Yeah, buildings in austere locations. Light bridges. Lots of
stuff.

CADET

Wow, I didn't know. That's pretty cool.

TODD

(Leans toward the Cadet.)

We also do logistics.

CADET

Logistics?

TODD

Yeah. We coordinate all the logistics, for our deployments.
You know what they say. Amateurs talk tactics. And
professionals…?

(Waits for the Cadet to reply.)

CADET

Talk logistics?

(Not fully sure of his answer.)

TODD

(Smiles and slaps the Cadet on the knee.)

You got it! Dude, you're a natural.

CADET

(Smiles and blushes, proud at receiving the
compliment.)

TODD

(Takes on an air of speaking in confidence.)

In fact, logistics are so important, that I've developed my own, personal logistics practice. (Beat.) Purely to grow my skills.

CADET

Personal practice? For logistics?

TODD

Yeah. Want to learn more about it?

CADET

Um, sure.

TODD

Great! (Beat.) Take you, for example. Where do you live? At school, I mean.

CADET

Um, I'm in an off-campus apartment.

TODD

(Nods.)

Off-campus apartment. That's good. That's very interesting. And, in this off-campus apartment, you have roommates?

CADET

Yes. There's four of us.

TODD

And for your neighbors, there's other college students?

CADET

Of course. Lots of them.

TODD

OK, this is good. You and your friends, you're pretty busy, right? Classes, extracurriculars, ROTC, college stuff. Pretty darn busy?

CADET

(Perplexed at where this is going.)
Uh huh, for sure.

TODD

And it's probably a pain to go and get all the stuff you need. For your apartment, I mean. Cleaning supplies, paper towels, toiletries, grocery stuff like cereal and sodas and chips. You're like, constantly having to go to the store. Right?

CADET

(Laughs.)
Yeah. We sort of play chicken. Me and my roommates. We get down to nothing, and then see who will break and finally go shopping.

TODD

Perfect! See, it's aa-llll logistics! (Beat.) *You* h*ave* a *need*. And thanks to logistics, you and I can solve it.

> (Turns to the laptop and toggles its display up to the big screen on the wall. He announces with a huge grin and gestures with his arm up to the wall monitor.)

Check out Sky-Way!

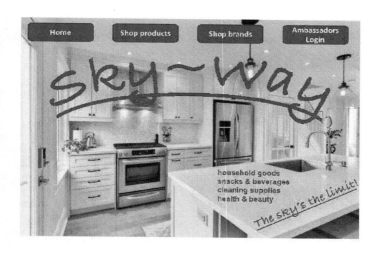

CADET

> (Squints, looking at the monitor.)

Sky-Way?

TODD

Yes, Sky-Way! The answer to all of your at-home logistics needs. Sky-Way can put *hours* back into your life, every month. Check it out!

    (Clicks through screens as he talks.)

It's a direct-market home products company that can *revolutionize* the way you think about shopping.

CADET

    (Leans forward to get a better look at the
    monitor.)

Sky-Way?

TODD

    (Nods his head and clicks to a new screen.)

Look at the home-cleaning products! Green, sustainable, competitively priced. All delivered *right to your door.*

    (Clicks to new screen.)

Need toiletries and health-care products? Sky-Way carries an industry-leading range of offerings. From name brand, to in-house generics. Whatever you want! And...

    (Slaps the Cadet lightly with the back of his
    hand, leaning toward him and smiling.)

Check. This. Out.

    (Clicks to next screen.)

All the snacks, sodas, canned goods and non-perishable food items you can dream of. Heck, you could live off Sky-Way entirely. No need for the grocery store!

CADET

So, I just order this stuff? Instead of going to the store?

TODD

Even better, I order it for you. As your franchise director.
And you get wholesale pricing as my subsidiary.
    (Pause.)
And dude, when we hook you up with your own franchisees,
on campus, the earnings can be huge. You and me, we can
go to town!

TOP

    (Enters from stage right. Looks up at the
    monitor.)

TODD

    (Frantically clicks off the display as he sees
    Top walk in.)

TOP

Todd, damn it! I laid down the law on this!

TODD

    (Hangs his head, looks at the floor. Speaks in
    a guilty voice.)
I'm sorry, Top.

TOP

Ain't no sorry! I laid down *the law* on this already.

TODD

(Looks up at Top. Speaks with a more clear, but still remorseful voice.)

I'm sorry, Sergeant.

TOP

(Stares at Todd in silence. Then speaks.)

You and I, *we w*ill take this up at another time. And in writing. Understood?

TODD

(Chastened.)

Understood, Top.

TOP

(Looks at his watch, then back to Todd.)

It is, right now, 0937 hours. In ten minutes I'm walkin' into that arms room. I'd better see you in there - showered, shaved, bustin' your ass to get us loaded out for the range tomorrow.

TODD

(Immediately rushes off stage left.)

TOP

(Grabs the coffee mug off his desk. Walks to refill at the coffee maker and returns to his own desk. While doing this, he's speaking to the Cadet, and at times shaking his head.)

Sir, the first rule of leadership on an A Team: Never keep 'em back in garrison for more than six weeks at a stretch. The young ones have too much time and energy on their hands. And that's when the trouble starts.

(Sits at his desk, facing the Cadet.)

Just like my kids. Too much time, plus too much energy, equals trouble.

CADET

(Nods solemnly.)

Understood, Top.

TOP

(Studies the Cadet for a moment.)

So, what do you think so far? About SF?

CADET

(Opens his mouth, but struggles at first to think of the right words.)

It's hard to say. (Beat.) So far this morning, I've been PT'd until I vomited. Got an IV like it was a party favor. Been a victim of online impersonation. Got caught up in the middle of the War of the Titans. Which, quite frankly, scared the hell out of me. And then sat through a hard-pitch for some Ponzi kind of business.

TOP

(Matter-of-fact voice.)

Just to be clear, and I've checked with the Battalion JAG on this, Sky-Way is technically a multi-level-marketing platform. *Not* a Ponzi.

CADET

(Looks at Top and cocks his head, confused.)

TOP

Meaning, Todd's business is fully legal. I don't approve of it, but it's legal. Now, sellin' it on team time, that's where I lay down the law. So, Mr. Todd and I, we're gonna put *that* in writing. He's gonna grow up or move out, fast.
    (Pause.)
But yeah, fully legal.

CADET

(Still flustered.)
But Top, all this stuff happened in my first *three and a half hours* with the team! Is it always like this?

TOP

(Pauses to consider.)
Noooo. You're right. This is sort of a slow mornin'.
    (He smiles at his own joke.)

CADET

(Guffaws.)

TOP

(In a sincere voice.)

Look, what questions you got? You're gonna be a commissioned officer. And believe it or not, an SF ODA is the ultimate leadership laboratory.

CADET

Well, my most pressing question is, will I survive PT tomorrow?

TOP

(Laughs out loud.)

CADET

Seriously. I thought I was going to *die*! Thank God for Doc giving me an IV.

TOP

Sir, you done fine. Just fine. The fellas won't tell you this, but more than one new guy has been dragged off their first Monster Monday with an IV in their arm.

CADET

Why do you do them? Monster Mondays.

TOP

(Reflects a moment. Looks more serious.)

This is a *good* team. We've got a good commander, too. But it's a young team. I'm the only one who's seen real combat. In Mogadishu, and in Panama before that.

CADET

(Listens intently.)

TOP

Monster Monday, every Monday. Not counting leave and holidays, that's north of forty Monster Mondays a year. The goal is not to train their bodies. I'm trainin' their brain stems.

CADET

(Digests this.)

Brain stems...

TOP

To you, PT this morning was a traumatic event. Overwhelming. To *them,* running the gauntlet like that is routine. Just showin' up for work after the weekend. When they're down range and takin' a real beating, it'll help 'em shrug off the physical pain. They'll have more mental energy available, to focus on winning the fight. (Beat.) Next question?

CADET

How are you going to handle the War of the Titans? Doc Hollins and Wes. It seems pretty bad between those two.

TOP

It's *Clash* of the Titans.
(Pause.)

An apt metaphor. Both Doc and Wes, they each see themselves as the Perseus of their own little world. So they fracas - over who gets to be Perseus.

CADET

Wes sure does seem angry. I'd call it more than a fracas. (Beat.) Which one of them do *you* think is Perseus?

TOP

My job's to make 'em all Perseus, in one way or another. (Beat.) Then I got to keep 'em off each others's backs. Or mostly at least. I heard about the arms room. Did Wes rough you up too bad?

CADET

(Shakes his head no.)

TOP

Well, you've got to know a little bit about Wes.

CADET

What's that?

TOP

Wes's grandma had a bad fall one night, when Wes was real little. Like three years old. His parents left him with one of the neighbors, while they rushed over to take care of her.

(He stops speaking. The silence resonates.)

CADET

And something happened? To the parents?

TOP

(Nods.)
Drunk driver killed both of 'em. It was a rough upbringing
for Wes, from then on.
(Pause.)
But he's makin' a good go of it, I'd say.

CADET

But it seems like those two, Wes and Doc, they're really
having a hard time working together.

TOP

Yeah, I've been thinking on that. (Beat.) We do combatives
on Fridays. Hand to hand combat. So far, I've been
intentionally keepin' those two apart. But now, it's time to
re-set the equilibrium.

CADET

It sounds like Wes will win. If you put them up against each
other?

TOP

Exactly. (Beat.) Wes will have Doc tapped out in about
twenty seconds. It'll be pretty brutal.

CADET

How is that equilibrium?

TOP

Look, Doc's a once-in-a-generation talent. But his poo stinks too. Wes chokin' him out will take Doc's ego down a notch. And it will calm Wes down some. Give him somethin' to hang his hat on.

         (Pause.)

Doc, he'll be all worked up for a bit. But then, maybe the next week, I'll remind him the silver lining, in Wes kicking his ass.

CADET

Silver lining?

TOP

         (Smiles. Leans forward.)

Wes is on our side. (Beat.) You *want* guys like that on our side.

CADET

         (Nods approvingly.)

TOP

When we head to the range tomorrow, we're stayin' in the field all week. Gonna run mounted and dismounted patrols through Friday morning. They issue you a ruck and full kit?

CADET

Yes. At least, I think they issued me everything.

TOP

Good. We report here tomorrow in full alert kit, and head out right after PT. Tell Mr. Todd I said to inspect your kit today, and for him to show you the team packing standard. He'll do you right. 'Cause he knows I'm gonna check, and it's his ass otherwise.

CADET

Will do. (Beat.) Where's Dai, um, where's the Captain?

TOP

He runs an extra four miles after team PT and then gets cleaned up. He'll be in the arms room by now, helping the fellas.

TOP

(Walks over to the coffee maker to refill.)
You ever shot a Mark-19 before?

CADET

(Looking enthusiastic.)
Negative!

TOP

(Nods.)

OK, why don't you go tell Jose you're gonna get a full can of ammo tomorrow. Ask him to give you a class on functions check and operations. He'll have you looking sharp for the range.

CADET

Thanks, Top!

(Exits stage right, smiling.)

(Fade.)

ACT [2]
SCENE [1]

> (The scene opens on the ODA
> 824 team room. The wall
> monitor reads 0820 hours on
> 9/11/2001.)

(All characters enter from stage right, in
sweaty PT gear.)

(Several of the following lines overlap, as two
or more team members speak
simultaneously.)

JOSE
(Grabs the Cadet by the collar bone. Smiles.)
See, no IV today.

CADET
Yeah! It wasn't Monster Monday. I'm just glad I got through!
(Top makes his way over to the coffee maker.)

DALE
(To Billy.)
We doing static fire all morning, or getting into immediate
action drills?

BILLY
(Response is inaudible against the background
noise.)

DOC
(Logs in at hot desk #1.)

WES
(To Todd.)
Hey man, I signed out a SOFLAM, too. Can you help out
with the class?

TODD
Sure thing. I was on the JTAC train up, right before you got
here.

TOP
(Standing at the coffee maker. Mug in hand.
Waiting for it to finish brewing.)
Listen up.
(They all stop talking and look to Top.)
Dai Uy's bustin' a move up to Battalion, to grab the range
book. Turn and burn on the showers. Work call at 0900,
with your field kit for the rest of the week. We'll roll out
right after that.

(The team members all reply more or less in
unison.)

                    JOSE

Roger.

                    BILLY

Roger that, Top.

                    DALE

Roger, Top.

          (Fade.)

ACT [2]
SCENE [2]

(The scene opens on the
empty ODA 824 team room.
The wall monitor clock scrolls
forward to 0857 hours on
9/11/2001.)

JOSE
(Walks in from stage left, in uniform and
carrying his field kit. The phone rings at
Top's desk. He sets down his kit and
answers.)
ODA 824. May I help you, Sir or Ma'am?
(Listens.)
Hey, Sir.
(Listens.)
Got it, Sir. I'll let Top know.

(As Jose hangs up, the rest of the team filter
in. They are also changed into field uniform.
They each carry their field kit, which they set
down throughout the room.)

TOP
(To Jose, gesturing toward the phone.)
What's up?

JOSE

That was Dai Uy. He says he's going to be late.

TOP

(Grunts.)

JOSE

Something about an accident in New York. A plane hit the World Trade Center or something. Dai Uy's having trouble getting the range book, because the Battalion Ops guys are all glued to the TV.

DALE

Oh, man.

> (Grabs the TV remote off hot desk #2. He points it to the wall monitor, intending to turn it on.)

TOP

> (Says with another grunt.)

Leave it. (Meaning, don't turn on the TV.) We've got a shit ton of rounds to shoot. Let's get loaded out. (Beat.) Dai Uy will catch up soon enough.

> (Dale sets the remote back on hot desk #2. The team exits stage right.)

> (The sound of footsteps fades. The team room sits empty for almost two minutes.)

(The phone on Top's desk begins ringing
again. It continues to ring incessantly. Finally,
off stage right, the sound of footsteps grows,
as someone runs back to the team room.)

TODD
(Appears on stage, irritated.)
What the hell.
(Picks up the phone receiver, and in a
professional voice.)
ODA 824. May I help you, Sir or Ma'am?
(Listens.)
Roger, Sir. (Beat.) OK, I'll get him ASAP. Roger. OK, OK,
yes, Sir!
(Bolts off stage right. Heard calling down the
hallway.)
Top!
(Pause.)
Hey, guys! It's important!
(Returns back on stage. Grabs the remote
from desk #5.)
(The rest of the team returns on stage.)

TOP
(Irritated.)
This had better be…

TODD

(Interrupts Top. At the same time, he's
turning on the TV wall monitor, looking for
a news report.)

Dai Uy says all hell broke loose at Battalion. There's been
another explosion in New York.

(A mix of concern and surprise shows on the
faces of the team members.)

TODD

(Finds a news report on the World
Broadcasting Service - or WBS - television
channel.)

JULIAN BURKE (WBS
Reporter)

(The news coverage opens in progress,
with WBS field reporter Julian Burke
giving on-scene reports from the World
Trade Center as footage plays on screen.)
(The footage replays a recent skyline
view of the Twin towers, with one tower
on fire and the other tower apparently
untouched.)
(Julian Burke's voice is in distress.)

Now, David, the video tape you're viewing is from just
moments ago. What you're seeing is a second plane
hitting the World Trade Center.

(Footage shows a passenger jet enter the
right side of the screen at high speed,
and impact with the second tower. A large
fireball explodes out the left side of that
tower.)

(Wes)

(In a flat, disbelieving voice.)

Holy shit.

JULIAN BURKE (WBS
Reporter)

These are horrifying pictures. I don't know how well
the footage showed the second plane. That also was an
airliner. Firefighters and EMS are already arriving in
large numbers. There's a tremendous amount of yelling
on the street, as first responders organize efforts and
as passersby take note. Many people are asking aloud
if, perhaps, there has been some breakdown in the air
traffic control system? If perhaps some navigation
error led to two impacts into the World Trade Center
within eighteen minutes of each other?

(Wide pan footage continues. Now, a much
larger, darker smoke cloud emanates
from where the second tower was hit.)

JOSE

(Shakes his head.)

That was no navigational error.

WES

(Nods, agreeing with Jose.)

Fuckin' A. That second plane was banking hard. Correcting course for an impact.

JULIAN BURKE (WBS
Reporter)

You say you have...? Sorry, that's the producers cutting in. They're rolling a new copy of that second airliner hitting the World Trade Center.

(A different video feed shows the impact of the second plane, from a slightly different angle. It clearly shows a two-engine passenger jet impacting at high speed.)

Again, this scene is just horrifying. Two catastrophic plane impacts, just eighteen minutes apart. We can't speculate or attribute the cause. But as I mentioned, some early chatter on the street is people asking if there has been some type of breakdown in the air traffic control system.

WES

Jose's right. That's no navigational error.

BILLY

(Speaking to Doc)

(All words are inaudible except.)...Stan?

DOC HOLLINS
(Shakes his head.)

I don't know.

JULIAN BURKE (WBS
Reporter)

You are looking at live pictures right now.
(The live picture now shows both towers,
with thick, dark smoke emanating from
the impact areas in each building.)

David, am I still with you?

DAVID STANSFIELD
(WBS Anchor)
(Stansfield is the national anchor for
WBS News, also based in New York. He is
leading the breaking news broadcast from
the WBS Midtown studios. Live footage
of the Twin Towers continues to play.)

You're still with us, Julian.

JULIAN BURKE (WBS
Reporter)

David, we're going off air momentarily. More fire
trucks are arriving, and a fire captain has just asked
that we reposition.

DAVID STANSFIELD
(WBS Anchor)

Understood, Julian. Thank you for these updates, and we will check back with you when you are on the air again.

> (The video feed switches to a reverse angle from before. A close-up shot fills the screen with the upper floors of the Twin Towers. This close-up makes clear the intensity of the fires that are burning.)

For those just joining us, you have been listening to live reporting on scene from WBS reporter Julian Burke. He is providing updates on this terrifying situation, ongoing now, at the World Trade Center in New York. Apparently two passenger jets, airliners, have impacted - one into the upper floors of each of the Twin Towers. For additional information, we bring in now another member of the WBS reporting team. We have just learned that our field reporter Sally Putnam has also arrived at the World Trade Center. Sally, over to you.

SALLY PUTNAM (WBS
Reporter)

Thank you, David. I've been on scene for about five minutes now. I was able to catch the end of Julian's broadcast. And that discussion at his location was about a possible failure in the air traffic control network. David, I have to tell you, I'm co-located with the NYPD Incident Commander. He is receiving initial reports from both the city Emergency Operations Center, and from FAA reports via that EOC.

> (She momentarily stops speaking, as loud sirens blare from a passing emergency vehicle.)

And what he is telling me is that there has <u>not</u>, again not, been any systemic control system failure that would lead to <u>two</u> coincidental crashes into each of the Twin Towers. While the Incident Commander is clear to specify that we do not yet have proof, authorities are now operating on the belief that this was a deliberate act.

TODD
> (Turns off the wall monitor. Says softly.)

Jesus.

> (Silence for several moments, with each team member in their own thoughts.)

DALE

Whoever did it will pay for this.

WES

Damn right. They'd better make sure of that.

TODD

(Nods.)

Yeah, they'd sure as hell better.

TOP

Jose, our range ammo, do we already have control of it? Secured in our CONEX?

(Dale looks at Top, confused at the question.)

JOSE

Roger that, Top.

TOP

Billy, our team equipment, for the field. You got our full SOP package uploaded in the DMVs, right?

BILLY

Of course, Top. Your standing guidance. Each time, every time, we carry our full contingency load.

WES

Top, what the hell? Our country's under attack, and we're still gonna roll to the field?

DALE

No shit, somebody needs to do something!

TODD

Fuckin' A they should.

TOP

(Stares at Wes, Dale, and Todd for a
moment.)

You're right. Someone should do somethin'.

(Pause.)

Welcome to the first day of earnin' your Tab. We're not
goin' to the field.

(It begins to register with them, what Top has
in mind.)

DALE

But...where? Who? We don't even know what this is about.

TOP

Not our job. Someone else'll figure out where, and who.
(Beat.) Our job, when they do figure that out. And trust me,
someone's gonna figure it out pretty darn quick. Any
operation this big leaves evidence. Lots of it.

(Pause.)

So, when someone does figure it out, our job is to be the first
ones in the barrel. I'll guarantee the BC and Group
Commander are thinkin' that way right now.

TODD

But it's that simple? For us to be first, I mean?

TOP

No, nothin's ever that simple. But showin' up and bein' ready at times like this, is the fastest way to get chosen.

BILLY

Top, we can work it from our end. But how do we get the nod for it to be us?

TOP

Well, there's eighteen teams in this battalion. But only one team is packed to go to the field, with a full contingency load, *right now*. And that same team happens to have its team commander pretty well positioned.

WES

Dai Uy! He's up there at Battalion, right now.

TOP

Correct. If I know Dai Uy, and I think I do, his radar's gonna be *finely tuned* for any mission requirements.

> (Jose and Billy nod. The rest of the team take in Top's assessment.)

> (Silence for several moments.)

> (The phone rings at Top's desk.)

TOP

(Walks over and picks up without any
greeting. The rest of the team move closer, in
a semi-circle, to possibly overhear. Top
listens, and replies.)

Sir. (Beat.) Yeah, we saw it. This ain't no accident. What's
the word up there?

(Dai Uy's voice is just barely recognizable on
the other end.)

Roger, that's a good call.

(Dai Uy speaks on the other end.)

You're damn right.

(Dai Uy speaks on the other end.)

OK, we're gonna get things moving here. Someone will stay
posted at this phone. Call in the updates as you get 'em.
(Beat). What are you thinking, N+4?

(Dai Uy speaks on the other end.)

Got it.

(Top hangs up.)

BILLY

(Gives a thumbs up, at hearing the N+4
reference.)

CADET

(Turns to Doc Hollins.)

N+4?

DOC HOLLINS

(Explains to the Cadet.)

Notification plus four hours. Meaning you're alerted to deploy. We might be getting busy.

TOP

The Battalion Commander and Ops Officer saw Dai Uy up there, and Dai Uy let 'em know our status. They already gave him a "hey you" to be ready. (Beat.) The B Team Commander and Sergeant Major are headin' up there now, to get the actual Warning Order. Dai Uy's gonna keep his ass planted there, to seal the deal.

JOSE

Top, you said N+4. Is that our planning factor, to start movement?

TOP

(Nods.)

For now. I'd even say, be ready to go faster than that. The loose talk is about pushin' out a pilot team. So, as soon as they find an air frame, we just might get the word to load up. (Beat.) Presuming we have a target country by then.

(The energy in the room grows noticeably focused, as the team members realize how quickly they will now need to prepare.)

TOP

Brief me your critical tasks. If we get the nod, we need to be self-contained once we go wheels up. Ain't gonna see no resupply for a while.

JOSE

(Looks at Wes and then back to Top.)
We've got our weapons prepped for the range. We can re-pack them now for air load out. (Beat.) Double basic load on ammo?

TOP

Triple basic load for small arms. Plus extra for functions tests and confirming zero. Plenty of sixty-millimeter mortar too, if you can find it.

TODD

(Looks at Billy.)
Billy, I can hit battalion for some logs plus-up. Maybe scare up maps if they have an AOR in mind?

BILLY

(Nods.)
Roger, do that. I'm going to the motor pool. If we go out as the pilot, we're probably setting up an ISB, too. We'll need three ISU-90s. Two at a minimum.

DALE

Same thing here. I'll hit SIGDET. Gonna twist some arms to plus us up for 117's. That should help Dai-Uy make the case, too, for us as a pilot.

TOP

Good. *Now* y'all are thinkin'. What else?

DOC HOLLINS

M-5 bags were packed and prepped for the range. I'll head to the med shed and scrounge up morphine, mefloquine, all the deployment plus-ups.

TOP.

(Looks at his watch.)

Alright, good start for now. It's 0913 hours. Go make initial contact in your lanes. Then get back here in forty-five minutes. (Beat.) We'll see what updates Dai Uy has.

(Team members filter out, until only Top and the Cadet are left in the room.)

CADET

What can I help with?

TOP

Why don't you man my desk, for when Dai Uy calls back.

(Pause.)

And think about anything we're missin' here.

CADET

But I don't know anything! I mean, you were in Mogadishu.

TOP

(Snorts.)

First law of combat. The last fight don't mean nothin'. Minute you get impressed with what you've done before, that's when some fifteen-year-old steps out of the shadows and shoots you in the face.

(The Cadet sits at Top's desk.)

TOP

What questions you have?

CADET

You talked about an "ISP"?

TOP

(Nods.)

It's "ISB." (Beat.) For Intermediate Staging Base. We'll need to put down on a lily pad and bring in the rest of the force. Organize. Then run our infil. To the actual target country.

CADET

Any ideas where? The ISB, I mean.

TOP

Well, it's usually some godforsaken airfield in the middle of nowhere.

(Pause.)

Main thing is to get you within helicopter striking distance. Or at least one fixed wing hop away.

CADET

And Dale was saying something about "117's"?

TOP

That's a better SATCOM radio. We've got the older version. The LST-5. SIGDET has a handful of the 117's. (Beat.) And right now, we need to be thinkin' about grabbin' the best capability we can. Across the board.

(Pause.)

You've done reading in ROTC. Amateurs talk tactics. And...?

CADET

Professionals talk logistics.

(Thinks for a moment, then laughs.)

TOP

What's so funny?

CADET

Todd used that logistics line on me yesterday. About Sky-Way.

TOP

Sky-Way, yes. Todd's about to get all the logistics he can handle. We're probably all about to get all we can handle.

CADET

(Thinks a little more.)

And that's why Monster Mondays, and other things like that.

TOP

And that's why Monster Mondays, and other things like that.

(Then recites a memorized quote.)

"Victory usually goes to the army who has the better trained officers and men."

CADET

Who said that?

TOP

A special operator if ever there was one. Sun Tzu.

(Looks at his watch.)

Well. Right now, *my* mission-critical task is to brew up a new pot. We've got a lot more things to figure out. (Beat.) Gonna pull another table in here too. Be right back.

(He grabs the coffee pot and exits stage left.)

(The Cadet sits alone, at Top's desk.)

(Fade.)

ACT [2]
SCENE [3]

(The scene opens on the ODA
824 team room. The wall
monitor clock scrolls forward
to 0956 hours on 9/11/2001.)

(The team huddles around a rectangular
planning table that Top brought in. Top
stands at the center of the table, facing the
audience. The Cadet is still seated at Top's
desk. The scene opens to background chatter
as team members exchange comments.)

(The phone rings at Top's desk.)

CADET
(Answers the phone in a low voice. His words
are initially inaudible due to the background
noise.)
...Thanks, Sir. (Pain shows in his face.) I'll let them know.
(He hangs up.)

(The team grows silent, and waits for the
Cadet's report.)

CADET

That was Dai Uy. Now the Pentagon's on fire.

TODD

Fuck.

DALE

(Picks up the TV remote, but looks to Top
for approval.)

TOP

(Nods his consent.)

DALE

(Clicks on the wall monitor to resume the
WBS news update.)

ELLIOT JACKSON (WBS
Washington Bureau Chief)
(The broadcast turns on with Jackson in
mid sentence.)

... not yet independently verified. What we are
watching live, ah, from Washington. We are witnessing
the Pentagon now on fire.

(An aerial video feed has zoomed in until
the Pentagon fills the screen. Thick,
dark-gray smoke emanates from the right
side of the building.)

We now have, in the nation's capital, what appears to be another significant explosion.

> (The video feed zooms in tight on the burning section and shows thick smoke billowing out at a rapid rate.)

If you are just joining, we are reporting on, ahhh, apparently another major blast. You are looking at live pictures of the Pentagon, with major structural damage and smoke visible. We cannot yet say if this was another airliner. We can say that following attacks on our financial center in New York, we now have an apparent attack on our, ah, center of national security at the Pentagon. This reported as of 9:43 Eastern Time Zone.

> (The screen now splits with the Pentagon feed on the right side, and a distance shot of the Twin Towers burning on the left side of the screen.)

We also have updates on the status of the President. President Bush is either in the air or shortly to be in the air, aboard Air Force One. He was at a school visit in Florida. The President has called this, quote, "An apparent terrorist attack on our country," this making official our operating assumption of the morning's events. We have word that Vice President Cheney is being moved to a secure, though undisclosed, location. Also, Reuters and the Associated Press have reports of hijacked airliners from American Airlines and United Airlines. We do not know how many hijacked airliners in total.

(The feed now goes single screen. It
alternates replays of the second plane
impacting the Twin Towers with various
angles of a current live feed in
Manhattan.)

Government officials report mass evacuations of major
federal buildings in DC. In New York, transit officials
report the closure of all regional airports, as well as
major bridges and tunnels. Ahh, and we now have
reports of new developments, possibly more explosions,
at Tower Two in New York. We will hand you over to
David Stansfield at our New York anchor desk for more
information.

(The feed cuts to David Stansfield in the
New York studio. He looks directly into
the camera.)

(The team members continue to watch
without speaking.)

DAVID STANSFIELD
(WBS Anchor)

Thank you, Elliot. This is WBS News coverage of
believed terrorist attacks this morning, both at the
World Trade Center in New York and now, apparently,
at the Pentagon in Washington.

(Pause.)

I think at this moment, I must share a phrase from my
longtime news colleague, Dan Rather. We began in local

news together in Texas, many years before becoming anchors at our respective networks. Among other things, we covered the JFK assassination. Dan's mantra at these times is "Steady... we must stay steady." We have tragic events unfolding in realtime. We also have precious little information about the actor or actors in these events.

> (The feed cuts back to various shots of
> the smoking Manhattan skyline.)

We will work diligently to separate fact from conjecture, even as our situation changes quickly. We are now back in communication with WBS field reporter Julian Burke. He is on scene at the World Trade Center. Julian, if you can hear us, I understand you have major updates at your location?

> JULIAN BURKE (WBS
> Reporter)
> (Skyline views continue of a smoke-filled
> Lower Manhattan. A wide-angle shot
> shows a new smoke cloud spreading
> rapidly away from the location of the
> towers, and then billowing upward. It
> appears that something significant has
> changed. Julian speaks with urgency in his
> voice.)

David (gasp), I'm calling you from an office building near the World Trade Center. I've lost track of my camera crew in the confusion, and am extremely concerned for their safety. The World... The top of one tower appears to have just disintegrated. (Gasp.) Whether it was another explosion, or the building itself coming apart, I do not know. But the entire top of the building collapsed down on itself. Debris, smoke, and dust spread violently on the street. Everyone had to just run, just flee for our lives.

(In the background, crying and shouting
echo from inside a large room.)

I found this phone here, in a ground-floor office in this building. You can see emergency responders outside, dazed but already trying to reorganize and help people. David, at this point I can't begin to speculate the loss of life. But we now have an even worse destructive event. We know we still had emergency workers and trapped office workers on the upper floors of that tower.

(More unintelligible shouting echoes in
the background.)

DAVID STANSFIELD
(WBS Anchor)

Julian, you said you're in a nearby office building. Where, exactly?

JULIAN BURKE (WBS
Reporter)
(His voice highly charged.)

David, I don't even know. The smoke, dust, and debris coming onto the street (gasp), I can only describe as violent and completely disorienting. I fear for my camera crew. Everyone just ran at top speed. I found this building and then called in to studio. I would say I'm two, maybe three blocks away from the Twin Towers.

                    BILLY
          (To Doc, in a very quiet voice that only Doc
          hears.)
I'm sure Stan's OK.

                 DOC HOLLINS
          (Gives a curt nod. Doesn't speak.)

               DAVID STANSFIELD
                (WBS Anchor)
          (Empathy in his voice.)
Julian, thank you for these difficult reports, even as you risk your safety and fear for the safety of your camera crew and those around you. We have you on live, as you are the best source of ground truth. Perhaps you have comment on other reports we are receiving, that it might be more than just upper floors that collapsed? That in fact one tower of the World Trade Center...
          (Julian Burke interrupts him.)

JULIAN BURKE (WBS
Reporter)
(More in control of his breathing now,
focused but urgent.)

Yes... no... David, your reports <u>are</u> correct. The collapse <u>started</u> with the upper floors. But it just kept coming down. At least the top third of the tower that I personally saw. But then we all had to flee. It was still coming down. David, I am fairly certain we have an entire tower down at this point.

TOP
(Says to Dale, softly.)

OK, Dale.

DALE
(Clicks off the remote.)

(The phone rings at Top's desk.)

CADET
(Answers the phone.)

Hello. (Beat.) Yes, Sir.
(Begins taking notes, very focused to ensure
he correctly captures information.)

Understood. Yes, Sir, I'll pass on the caveats, too. (Beat.) I think so. But wait one, Sir.
(Holds the phone out to Top.)

                    TOP

          (Grabs the receiver, looking to the Cadet for
          context.)

                   CADET

They're pushing up the timeline. He wants to know if you
can make it.

                    TOP

Sir?
          (Listens.)
Yes, Sir. (Beat.) We can make that. Tell the Old Man we're
tracking. (Beat.) Is your kit all packed?
          (Listens.)
OK, we'll load it on the pallet. (Beat.) See you at A/DACG.
(Pronounced "ay-dag.")

          (He hangs up the phone.)

                    WES

          (Hits Todd on the arm.)

Fuckin' A.

                   CADET

          (Asks Dale, in quiet voice.)

A/DACG?

                    DALE

Airfield Departure and Control Group. The departure
terminal on post.

JOSE

We're going, Top?

TOP

(Nods.)

The Group S-3 is about to hop a C-141 to go scout an ISB.
The Group Commander told Battalion, if an ODA's ready
to fly out by then, put 'em on it.

JOSE

What's showtime?

TOP

N+3:30.

TODD

(Whistles.)

Damn, Top. You know how to call it.

TOP

We're trackin', right?
                (He scans the team.)
We can make it, right?

JOSE

It's tight. But we can make it. (Beat.) Any other updates,
from Dai Uy?

TOP

That's all I heard.

(To the Cadet.)

What else did he have, when you were talking to him?

CADET

He said that - *Battalion S-2 says* - based on previous reporting, it's almost surely Al Qaeda behind the attacks.

(He pauses, careful to repeat the phrasing

exactly as he heard it.)

And. According to the *S-2*. That means it's probably Afghanistan. The target country will probably be Afghanistan.

(The team members all look to Top.)

TOP

That makes sense. OK, we ain't got much time. (Beat.) But let's talk through any last-minute mods we need to make.

(To Dale.)

We're gonna be comms heavy. You got the 117's *and* our LST-5's?

DALE

(Nods.)

Roger, Top.

TOP

Good.

(Pause.)

Afghanistan. That's a lot of *wide open* terrain.

JOSE

Some long engagements. Who you want on the sniper system?

TOP

Our best shot.
        (Looks to Doc.)
Doc, you'll carry the M24.

WES

        (Huffs, angry that he's not chosen.)

DOC HOLLINS

        (To Wes.)
BSC has one of the guns chambered for .300 Win Mag, in their arms room. That's four hundred meters extra range. Why don't you go sign that out for us?

WES

Motherfucker, you're not my boss!

TOP

Not *now,* Wes!

DOC HOLLINS

Well, maybe I *should* be!

TOP

God damn it, Doc! Mister, you'd better put that ego of yours in check. Clear?

                    DOC HOLLINS
          (Chastened at the rebuke.)
Sorry, Top.

                        TOP
          (Normal voice now, but in a slightly scolding
          tone.)
Both of you, we ain't got time to waste.
          (To Doc.)
Doc, we all know weapons ranges on this team. No one
needs you givin' a lecture. Clear?

                    DOC HOLLINS
          (Nods in acknowledgment.)

                        TOP
          (To Wes, in a supportive tone.)
Wes, he's right. When we break huddle, get over to BSC and
grab that .300 Win mag. Don't take no for an answer. Clear?

                        WES
          (Past his emotion. Focused on the task.)
Clear, Top. I'm on it.

                        TOP
Alright. By the new timeline, we're at N+30 minutes now.
At N+2:30 we need to be rolling out of here to A/DACG.
(Beat.) What are our other mission criticals?

JOSE

The weapons and triple basic load are good to go. We can have them loaded in an hour.

TOP

The more I think on it, if we have room, fill up the rest of that ISU with ammo and batteries.
            (Looks to Billy.)
How many ISU-90s we get?

BILLY

They assigned us two. But we've also got that old one, the empty one we were about to turn in. I'll snag that as a third. (Beat.) We'll load in a GP Medium, two weeks MREs, and any medical plus-ups that Doc wants. We'll still have some fudge room left.

TOP

            (Lost in thought for a moment.)
Damn. Wherever we drop that ISB, sure enough it's gonna be in *nowheresville*. Wish we could stock up with more than MREs. Like coffee, and some honest to goodness toilet paper. At least stuff to get us started.

TODD

Top! I got it all covered. TP, coffee, coffee filters, snacks, you name it!

TOP

(Studies Todd for a second.)

Well, for once I'd approve of Sky-Way. (Beat.) But we're outta time. There's no way you can run home to your stash and get back here.

TODD

No! It's already, I got it…

(Stops at realizing what he's about to admit.)

TOP

Todd.

(Pause.)

Where is your Sky-Way stash?

TODD

(Looking down.)

I've been keeping stuff in that old ISU. The same one Billy's talking about. (Beat.) Figured it wasn't bothering anyone, since we were about to turn it in. It helped me make deliveries faster.

(Looks up at Top. Bracing for his reply.)

TOP

(In a flat voice.)

Well, Todd.

(Pause.)

We got two engineer sergeants on this team. And Billy can fly solo no problem.

(Pause.)

So, I think, I think we're just gonna leave you back here to focus on your day job, at Sky-Way. And the rest of us will head out and do *our* day job.

TODD

(Horrified.)

No, Top. Please don't leave me back!

(Grows more quiet, but extremely serious.)

I couldn't live with myself, not to go on this.

TOP

(Looks at Todd in silence for several seconds.)

You're gonna *donate* all that crap, out of your own pocket.

TODD

(Nods vigorously. Extreme relief shows.)

TOP

And Todd. When we get back, *if* we come back; no more Sky-Way. (Beat.) This is where you become all growed up. Got it?

TODD

(Nods vigorously again. More relief.)

Roger, got it. Thanks, Top! I won't let you down.

TOP
(Looks at his watch, addresses the entire
team.)
Alright. It's time to execute. (Beat.) First priority, everyone
get on a cell phone or use a line in the B Team. Take twenty
minutes to call your family. Don't know the next time we'll
get a chance. Then get on your tasks, and we'll rally at
A/DACG.

(Jose and Dale are the first to file out, exiting
stage right. As team members depart, they
shoulder their individual kit and carry it out
with them.)

(Billy and Todd compare notes. Then they
also walk toward the stage right exit.)

CADET
(Calls to Billy and Todd before they leave the
room.)
You need any help?

BILLY
Absolutely, we can use another set of hands. C'mon.
(Billy and Todd exit stage right.)

CADET
(Starts to walk out, to join them.)

WES

(Grabs the Cadet by the arm.)

Hey, dude. They won't let you onto the airfield, when you get to A/DACG. So, in case I don't see you, sorry for almost kicking your ass.

CADET

(Nervous smile, still uncomfortable at the memory of the episode.)

No problem. I'd have been pissed, too.

(More solemn.)

Good luck.

WES

Thanks. But it's the other side that better be praying for luck. They don't know what's coming.

CADET

(Nods in agreement, then exits stage right.)

WES

(To Doc.)

I'll get that gun for you.

(Exits stage right.)

(Top and Doc are now the only two left in the team room.)

TOP
(As he speaks, also collects papers from the
work table.)
Doc, you'd better get a move on.

DOC
(Grabs the remote. Clicks on the TV.)
I need to check the latest.

(The broadcast opens to the WBS news
coverage, with field reporter Sally
Putnam reporting on scene at the World
Trade Center. She speaks into the
camera.)

SALLY PUTNAM (WBS
Reporter)
... moved from the immediate vicinity of the Twin
Towers, following the collapse of the South Tower
some twenty five minutes ago. And David, there is
another alarming development that we must relay to
you.
(Pause.)
Throughout the morning, there have been many, many
instances of people falling from the upper floors of the
Twin Towers onto the street, in yet another horrifying
layer on this morning of national tragedy. We cannot
know for certain if this has been people jumping, to
escape the intense heat and flames on the upper floors,

or if people are slipping and falling while trying to escape past damaged and blocked areas. But even before the fall of the South Tower, it caused Fire and EMS officials to begin expanding their safety cordon around the Towers.

(The scene cuts back to a skyline view of the North Tower, which is understood at this point to be the only tower that still stands. Heavy smoke continues to flow from the North Tower.)

DAVID STANSFIELD
(WBS Anchor)
(The camera feed remains with live coverage of the North Tower and surrounding area, as Stansfield gives commentary.)

Sally, we know how difficult this has been, for both you and Julian, while providing coverage on scene. As you so rightly say, this is a morning of national tragedy. For viewers who may just be joining us, we now have confirmed attacks on American soil. In New York, the World Trade Center towers have been deliberately hit by passenger airliners. The South Tower has recently collapsed. At the Pentagon, in Washington, we have had a large explosion and fire. As precautionary measures, both the White House and the Capitol have been evac...

(The live video feed of New York now
shows the top of the North Tower
collapsing and disappearing into a dense
cloud of dust and smoke.)

And now what you are viewing, live - the upper stories
of the North Tower are also now collapsing.

(At least half the tower appears to
disintegrate.)

The tragedy of it.

(The anchor pauses. Dust continues to fill
the video frame. Sirens can be heard
amidst cityscape background noise.)

One simply cannot make sense of this. (Pause.) What
you are watching are large portions of the North Tower
collapsing in on itself. Through the rising smoke, we can
see at least some part of the structure, the Tower, still
intact. It's the right side of the Tower from our
vantage point, perhaps one half or more of its full
height.

(That remaining right-side portion of the
Tower stands alone for several moments,
then it too collapses.)

We also have confirmation that President Bush is
airborne from Sarasota, Florida. This follows a visit he
was conducting this morning at the Emma E. Booker
Elementary School. Where the President is en route to,
we do not yet know. We know that the Vice President
has been removed from his West Wing office to a
secure, though undisclosed, location. And from the

vantage point on our live view of the World Trade Center, we now have this newest development - the collapse of the North Tower.

> (A wide pan shot shows that neither of the Twin Towers is standing any longer.)

As our WBS colleague Sally Putnam has said while reporting on scene at the World Trade Center, we will remember this as a morning of national tragedy.

                    DOC HOLLINS
            (Clicks the remote to turn off the TV.)

                        TOP
Doc, you'd better get a move on. We ain't got much time.

                    DOC HOLLINS
Top, I need to go *home*. Not call.

                        TOP
                (With some edge.)
Don't tell me you left some loadout gear? We should *already* be going to the airfield.

                    DOC HOLLINS
            (Perturbed at that suggestion.)
No. My gear's all…it's not that.
                    (Pause.)
Stan. (Beat.) Natalie's brother.

TOP

(Looks away, making the connection. Then
looks back.)

Shit. Doc. Was he on shift this morning?

DOC HOLLINS

No idea.

(Pause.)

But he's Ladder Company 3. They would've been one of the
first responders on scene.

TOP

(Looks down, thinking. Looks at his watch.)

Doc, look. We're on a quick turn here.

(Pause.)

You don't even know Stan's status. And you know the
Group standard. We're non-deployable without a medic. If
you miss showtime, at the airfield, they'll kick the whole
team off the bird. (Beat.) We need to make our phone calls
from here, load out, and go.

DOC HOLLINS

(Holding firm.)

Top.

TOP

(With heightened emphasis.)

Doc. (Beat.) That's *just* the way it has to be.

(They each look at the ground for a moment,
then Doc looks up.)

DOC HOLLINS
(In a quiet tone, almost pleading.)
Top, Stan's dead. I just know it. I *need* to go home and say
goodbye to Natalie, and give her at least that.

(A more lengthy pause as Top thinks it
through.)

TOP
You got ninety minutes. Then get your ass on that bird.

DOC HOLLINS
Thanks, Top. I'll never forget this.

TOP
You'd better get goin'. Tell Natalie we'll all be prayin' for
Stan.

DOC HOLLINS
Thanks, Top. I will.
(Exits stage right.)

TOP
(Alone now. Looks around one last time, for
any items the team might have forgotten to

load out. Then grabs his kit and exits stage
right.)

(**Fade.**)

ACT [2]
SCENE [4]

> (The scene opens on the ODA
> 824 team room. The wall
> monitor clock scrolls forward
> to 0200 hours on 4/11/2002.)

B TEAM OPS NCO
> (His voice is off stage, to stage right. He is
> never visible in the team room.)

Damn, you drove straight through? How long did that take?

CADET
> (The Cadet's voice is also off stage to stage
> right. He sounds somewhat weary.)

Yeah. About eleven hours.

B TEAM OPS NCO

How'd you know to head down here?

CADET

I saw a news report the first teams were coming home.

B TEAM OPS NCO

Well, you timed it just right. (Beat.) They're landed. BSC is
trucking 'em over from A/DACG right now.

CADET

(Steps on stage, still looking at the B Team
Ops NCO offstage.)

How are they?

B TEAM OPS NCO

They had a tough go, but they did a good job.

CADET

Are they all OK?

B TEAM OPS NCO

I guess not all the news reports made it up your way. The
team's pulling up to the building now. (Beat.) Give 'em
some space. I'm sure they'll appreciate you driving down.

CADET

(Surveys the team room in silence.)

(Jose, Billy, Todd, and Dale walk in. They
each carry kit, which they set down. Though
they are surprised to see the Cadet, their
overall emotion is flat.)

JOSE

(Shakes hands with the Cadet.)

Sir, we didn't expect to see you. Thank you for coming to
greet us.

BILLY

(Also shakes hands.)

Hey, it's great to see you.

(Todd and Dale are further away, and say
almost in unison, "Hey, man.")

CADET

How's, um. (Beat.) How's everyone else?

BILLY

Top's down the hall at the B Team. He'll be here in a few.

JOSE

Dai Uy's up at Battalion, to report our return to the CQ.
(Silence hangs in the room.)

CADET

(From their tone, the Cadet realizes that Doc
and Wes are not with the team, and the
possible implications of this.)

(Jose logs on to the computer at hot desk #1.)

(Billy steps out to grab more kit. He walks
back in and sets it down.)

DALE

(Seems preoccupied, agitated. He grabs a clip
board with an inventory sheet.)

Call out sensitive items as you unpack. I'll log them in. So
we can get the hell out of here.

TODD

(Also looks preoccupied. He stands in silence
for some moments. Then blurts out.)

They should fire Dai Uy's ass!

DALE

(Nods.)

You're damn right they should.

JOSE

It's not that simple.

TODD

Not that simple? We got completely overextended! How can
it not be that simple?

DALE

Todd's right, man.

(Pause.)

We're lucky any of us got out alive.

JOSE

(More stern now.)

I'm telling you. (Beat.) It's not that simple.

TODD

You keep saying that. Well, it looked pretty fucking simple
to me, Jose.
                    (Pause.)
It looked to me like *the Cadet* here would've recognized that
we were about to have a tsunami drop down on us.

DALE

No joke.

TODD

                    (Still looking at Jose.)
And Dai Uy, he just kept us charging on in. Charging on in.

DALE

Jose, like I said, we're lucky for any of us to be alive.
                    (Looks to Billy.)
What do you think?

BILLY

                    (Hesitates a moment.)
Look, the situation sucked. I get that. But I'm with Jose.

TODD

Be whoever you want to be with. Dai Uy should get his ass
fired! It *is* that simple.

TOP

(Enters from stage right. He's immediately on
edge at hearing the tail end of the discussion.)

Who's talkin' about gettin' who fired?

TODD

(Looks down. Doesn't speak.)
(More silence in the room.)

TOP

Todd. You were shootin' your mouth off real good there.
(Pause.)

Let's hear it again. Who needs to get who fired?

TODD

(Intimidated, but his frustration breaks
through.)

Damn it, Top! You know what I'm talking about. We all
knew we were overextended. Fighting down that final set of
ridge lines. We heard you! Calling it out.

TOP

And?

TODD

And? No and! We should have set up, brought in more air,
something. (Beat.) We shouldn't have just kept pushing. We
could all see it changing.

TOP

(Laser focused and in control, but with edge
in his voice.)

I see your point. We should'a just quit?

(Pause.)

Just quit, and gone home.

TODD

That's not what I'm saying, and you know...

(Top cuts him off.)

TOP

(Quiet but forceful.)

That's exactly what you're saying.

(Pause.)

Who are you talkin' overextended? We were overextended
for the whole deployment.

(Looks at Dale.)

Dale, I heard you shootin' some sabot rounds, too?

DALE

(Uncomfortable at being singled out. Doesn't
speak.)

TOP

No, how about it, Dale? You feelin' a little overextended?

DALE

Well, Top...I...

(He lapses into silence.)

TOP

Yeah, sort of hard when you're on the spot to give an answer.

(Pause.)

When did we get overextended? (Beat.) That ain't rhetorical.
Someone tell me. When did we get overextended?

(Pause.)

BILLY

As soon as we left Camp Diamond, Top.

TOP

Damn straight.

(His initial edge toned down. Now trying to
help his guys process the context of their
combat losses.)

We loaded outta' here in nothin' flat. And we started
runnin'. And we didn't stop until we took Kabul.

(Pause.)

With nothin' but a handful of special operators, air when we
could get it, and - God bless 'em - the tribes that joined our
side.

TODD

(Now in a more subdued mix of anger and
sadness.)

But Top, we knew how sketch it was getting, that day.
(Beat.) Going down that hillside.

TOP

Maybe. Looking back always feels sketchy, when that's
where you lost your guys.
(Pause.)
We led three big-ass assaults before pushin' down that ridge
line. (Beat.) Every one of them was a cluster. Right?

JOSE

Roger that.
(Silence in the room.)

TOP

Plus the other firefights. (Beat.) Dai Uy had to make a fast
call every time. Flank left, flank right. Attack right away and
aim for surprise? Or hold up and if - if we could get some air
– use that first.
(Pause.)
And you know the deal. When Group couldn't get the air in
time. When Bossman didn't have anything in orbit. Then
sometimes it made sense to charge in, surprise or not.

DALE

But what was the status, Top? That day? Were we completely
out of options, to get air support first?

TOP

(Shakes his head.)

We're not even goin' there. (Beat.) You fight the fight, and lead the tribals. I keep the team in the fight. (Beat.) As fast as things were moving that day, Dai Uy had to sort it out with Bossman and make the call.

(Pause.)

If we replayed the invasion twenty times from start to finish. Most every time, we'd have at least two of us dead. And some of those times, we'd have more than that.

(Silence.)

DALE

(With pain in his voice.)

Doc and Wes were good men.

TOP

(Empathetic.)

Yes, they were. They were two of the best.

TODD

And Natalie. Losing Stan first, and then losing Doc.

(Silence.)

TOP

It's awful for Doc's family. They'll live with this forever.

(Pause.)

But as awful as that is, this is the job we signed up for. It was our job to be on that ridge. There's a reason the taxpayers pay for us. They pay for us to be the only ones in this country who could fly out on no notice, embed with a disorganized tribal army, and then win the fight.

> (Pause.)

And check it out. We ain't done. I've been in small wars. Somethin' says this one ain't gonna stay small.

> (The phone rings at Top's desk.)

TOP

> (Picks up and listens.)

Sir? Yes, Sir. Be right up there.

> (Looks to the team.)

Battalion wants to see all the team leadership, before they release us. Sounds like it'll be pretty quick.

> (Departs stage right.)

> (Silence in the room for a few more moments.)

TODD

I still don't know. I don't know. It just felt reckless, making that last push.

DALE

> (Nods.)

I'm inclined to agree.

JOSE

(Shakes his head.)

Top's right. The whole invasion was reckless, but *necessary*.
(Beat.) That last assault was just another part of winning the fight.

BILLY

Like Top said, we gotta move past it. He's right about
another thing. I don't think we're done.

(Todd and Dale still look pained.)

DALE

It was just…those two always goin' at it. They couldn't stand
each other.

JOSE

I know.

BILLY

Wes always was a brawler. He would have thrown down,
regardless. Whoever was stuck out there.

DALE

But those last few minutes.

(He stops abruptly. A hint of tears showing in
his eyes.)

JOSE

I know.

(More silence in the room.)

CADET

(After a spell, asks respectfully.)

What happened?

(The four team members all seem to wait, to
see who will speak first.)

DALE

We landed in Nuristan, and started pushing south. Down
into Kunar.

JOSE

The tribal link up was a total goat rope. But the main thing
we had in our favor, was the Taliban were in even more
confusion, at least at first. The Air Force had beat them up
pretty badly.

BILLY

Like Top said, we were getting in some big fights. *Completely*
wild.

(Pause.)

Our team partnered with just over four hundred tribals.
Total chaos, working with them.

JOSE

It's not their fault. They just have no training. All self-
taught, from the Muj days right down until today. So they
spray and pray. They're brave fighters as individuals. But as
a group, they're unpredictable.

DALE

We got in big fights in Nuristan, and in Kunar. It all went our way. Dicey a couple of times, but we got some air to break the Taliban's momentum. That was usually the tiebreaker - the air.

BILLY

That final push was to Jalalabad. The bad guys started getting desperate. Once we took J'bad, the door to Kabul was wide open. You're not bottled up anymore.

JOSE

From J'bad, you punch straight west through the plains. (Beat.) Or head southwest to Gardez and buttonhook up.
(Pause.)
And we had other teams moving in from the north, toward Bagram. It was setting up a double envelopment.

DALE

Yeah, the Taliban knew this was their last holdout. Or else it's "Kabul's gone and game over." So they were playing for keeps, when we came down from that last mountain pass.

BILLY

Things started out OK, pushing down the ridge. We had the tribals organized in three companies. Spread abreast on an assault line.
(Pause.)

The ridge we were on. The one leading to J'bad. It started to flatten out. So we spread each company out a lot more. Then the Taliban in front of us just *melted away*. Gone. There were tall hilltops on either side of us. Couldn't see to our left or right, with those flanking hills blocking our view.

TODD

It *totally* didn't feel right.

JOSE

You *can't* say that now. None of us jumped on the net. None of us yelled out, "Hey, stop!"

TODD

What the hell are you talking about? Top was on there saying, "Watch the flanks" like, every *ten seconds*.

JOSE

Top said, "Watch the flanks" on *every* assault.

TODD
(Shakes his head.)
Not like that! We were all swiveling our heads like crazy. (Beat.) Everyone could tell that something was different.

BILLY

Cut it out.

TODD

We just gambled that we'd race in to J'bad and be the big heroes.

BILLY

Cut it out!

(Silence.)

DALE

(To the Cadet.)

And then they sprung the trap on us. Right as we got down on the lower part of that ridge. Where it flattened out into a broad slope, flanked by those hills on either side.

BILLY

It had to be two thousand total. A thousand from behind each hilltop. They hit our left and right flank companies simultaneously, like freight trains.

DALE

And the rockets. They rocketed the hell out of our center company.

(Pause.)

In a heartbeat, we ceased to function as a combat formation. Some of the Muj were wounded or killed. The rest just fought the way they always have - haul ass if it gets that bad. They just all hauled ass.

CADET

What happened to you guys?

JOSE

You have to understand. We were loaded down so heavy, compared to our tribal partners. We had SATCOMs, a SOFLAM, thermals. You can't just drop all that gear and run.
(Pause.)
We had three of us with the right-side company. And three of us in the center.

BILLY

It was fluid. On the team, we were mix-and-matching in with the companies all day. (Beat.) When the tsunami hit, Wes and Doc were paired with that left-hand company.

DALE

The tribals just un-assed.
(Pause.)
Dai Uy ordered our team to rally back up the ridge line, about seven hundred meters. (Beat.) That put us onto a spur we could defend long enough to call in air support.

JOSE

It was a madhouse. We were so overrun at that point, we weren't *retreating*. We were assaulting to the rear, up that ridge line to the spur.

BILLY

There was so much hitting at once, it was everyone fighting solo for about five minutes. Hell, three of us survivors got Purple Hearts that day. (Beat.) We finally got onto that spur and took a count.

TODD

It wasn't Wes's fault! God damn him. Why did he blame himself?

BILLY

We got up there. We had the whole team except Doc. (Beat.) During all of Wes's fighting, up from where that left-hand company got hit, Wes thought *he* was bringing up the rear. He thought Doc was uphill of him the whole time.
> (Pause.)
But it turns out, Doc had gone down wounded, right away. He never moved ten feet.

DALE

From the spur, Top spotted Doc with our thermals, still down there. And by then that part of the ridge was crawling with Taliban. (Beat.) Wes went apeshit at realizing he'd left without Doc. Went totally apeshit. He was yelling for us to immediately assault back down there.

JOSE

It would have been suicide. It *was* suicide.

BILLY

Dai Uy and Top called for ECAS, air, to hit the biggest clump of Taliban down there. (Beat.) They yelled orders to wait for the air strike. There were too many Taliban.

DALE

But Wes was looking through his optics too, at Doc's position. He did the math. Some of the Taliban would find Doc before the ECAS could push 'em back.

TODD

(Just shakes his head.)

BILLY

Wes took off. Hauled ass back down that ridge line. Dai Uy and Top yelled like crazy for Wes to stop. (Beat.) Wes never even slowed down.

JOSE

A dust cloud rolled in, and you couldn't make out what happened. When we finally got down there, we found the bodies of seven of their fighters - all within twenty feet of Doc.

CADET

What about the air strike?

DALE

The air strike hit right on target. Danger close, three-hundred-fifty meters away from Doc's position. It wiped out a few dozen Taliban. (Beat.) Their survivors all fled.

JOSE

Our team launched as soon as the bombs impacted.
　　　(Pause.)
We reached Doc's position just a couple of minutes later.

BILLY

Dai Uy and Top were scared shitless for Wes. That he might have been caught in the impact zone for the bombs.

CADET

Was he?

BILLY
　　　(Shakes his head.)
No, no. We got down to Doc's position, and Wes was right there with him. (Beat.) Doc was dead. Wes was alive and conscious, but had taken three rounds through his right leg. He had bled out bad. Femoral bleeder.

TODD

Fucking Wes.

JOSE

Dai Uy called a medevac. But we all knew the deal. Wes did, too. There was almost no way a medevac could get in there and back to the CASH in time. We got a tourniquet and IV going ASAP. Wes was almost out by then.

BILLY

Top knelt down next to Wes. Top was beside himself, knowing he was gonna lose Wes, too. He chewed Wes out for disobeying orders. He said, "You shouldn't have done that! Now we might lose both of you. It wasn't worth it."
(Pause.)

DALE

(Sad, but smiles at the memory of what Wes said next.)

And then old Wes, he looked up and said, "But Top, it was worth it. (Beat.) Because when I got to Doc, he was still alive - barely. Doc just smiled and said, 'Wes, I knew you'd never leave me.'"

TODD

We had to watch him die, Wes. We never stopped working on him. The MH-47 that ran medevac, it redlined it the whole way. It was just too far to move him, with not enough time.

CADET

(Nods solemnly.)

(The team stands in silence.)

131

TOP

(Enters from stage right.)

Alright, listen up.

(The team gives Top their attention.)

Got some updates from Battalion.

(Pause.)

Jose and Billy, congratulations. You got yourselves fired.

CADET

(Confused at what this means.)

TOP

You're each getting your own teams. Tomorrow morning, 0800 hours, report to the Battalion CSM. He'll tell you which companies you're going to.

JOSE

Roger, Top.

BILLY

Thanks for the vote of confidence, Top.

TOP

Well, don't go screwin' up and makin' an ass of me, got it?

(Jose and Billy each smile, though subdued from the recent discussion about Doc and Wes.)

JOSE

Solid copy, Top. We'll do you right.

TOP

Dale and Todd, you're my seniors now. (Beat.) I'm gonna be leanin' on both of you, askin' you to carry a heavy load.

(Dale and Todd stand up straighter at hearing this.)

DALE

Roger that, Top.

TODD

Roger, Top. We'll get it done.

TOP

I know you will.

TOP

(To the Cadet.)

Sir, I appreciate you driving down to welcome us back. Normally, I'd say stick around and finish your two weeks. But we've got briefings tomorrow. We'll get some leave. And after that, it's right back into the mix.

CADET

I understand.

(Pause.)

BILLY

What goes tomorrow, Top?

TOP

Battalion's issuing a warning order. (Beat.) Gears are already turnin' for our next deployment.

DALE

Damn, back to Afghanistan already?

TOP

(Shakes his head.)

No. Not Afghanistan.

(Pause.)

We're prepping for Iraq.

(Looks of confusion and surprise show among the team members.)

(Fade.)

A Note from Bill

Thank you for your purchase of *The Team Room*, and thanks for exploring three days in the life of ODA 824. In 21st century publishing, reader reviews play an outsized role for growing an audience. If you have a few moments to leave a rating or review, either on the purchase website or on any platform of choice, I will be forever grateful.

Contact events@billraskin.com to request speaking engagements or for options to license performances. If you want to directly share any thoughts on the play, please reach out to bill@billraskin.com. Also, visit billraskin.com for additional articles and information on my novel, *Cardiac Gap*.

Some notes on the play (**spoiler alert**):

This story is full of lies. My mates from the special operations community will recognize that straight off. It employs made up characters from a long-extinct Special Forces Group, based at a fictitious Army post. It also distorts time and scale – covering a wide range of vignettes with just nine characters and an hour and change of stage time. For that reason, I chose 9/11 as the anchor event. The bigger the crisis, the more the accelerant and impact. I am struck at how those days in late 2001 continue to shape our world in major ways.

Telling lies aside, all fiction borrows from the real world.

For example, the 5th Special Forces Group's early deployments to Afghanistan are rightfully the stuff of legend. I deployed with a different unit on the 9/11 response, entering the Afghan combat zone right after Thanksgiving, 2001. Though serving outside the SF Regiment by that point, I was no less amazed at the unique impact that an A Team brings to the modern battlefield. In later years I had the chance to culminate my active duty with 5th Group, and will always cherish that experience.

The stateside vignettes also benefitted from real-world inspiration. Everyone who works around military free-fall has tales of calamity or near-calamity, such as befell Dai Uy in the story. That skill is a necessary but high-risk endeavor. And years ago, I recall some retired special operators trading laughs about a bear that had left footprints through their patrol base. (Wish I could remember who - if it's *you*, please do drop a note!) I merged these with other career experiences, to try and capture the brilliance of Army collaborative leadership. Officers command, while non-commissioned officers advise and share authority to supervise/lead. It is an uncommon arrangement, but one that makes all services of the US military that much stronger.

One vignette that derived from an old classic: The final scene episode of Wes returning to Doc's aid, and dying in the process. This plays on an often shared but elusively sourced anecdote about military friendship. Across many different forums it's been attributed to either two soldiers or two Marines, in World War I or World War II, and to various authors or originators. Most often, variations are attributed to Leslie D. Weatherhead (b. 1893, d. 1976). Weatherhead was an English theologian who published several dozen books throughout his life. Regardless of the source, the legend offers great commentary on the bonds of soldiering. I wanted to work it into an updated theme here. In the tight confines of a team, head-butting can and does occur at times. But an external drama will generally wash that away, quickly, and often leaves a good friendship remaining.

As a writing project, this began with intent to create a short story anthology. But the early drafts didn't find their groove. It then coalesced into a stage play, and that felt more appropriate. In the ecosystem of high-performance teams, interpersonal dynamics become the daily life blood. I ultimately just wanted to get out of the way and let the characters do the talking. I hope that succeeded.

In the relative scheme of the special operations community, this play depicts a "young" team. That is to say, several of the characters are new to the force. Some are still adjusting to what this life means to them, or at least, what it came to mean to me. Young teams also tend to need more personal mentoring from their team leadership. And, of course, the pre-9/11 atmosphere was a less existential time for those serving in combat arms units. A long way of saying, most of the time the atmosphere in special operations runs pretty routine and business-like. My novel, *Cardiac Gap*, aimed to capture more of the seasoned operators and just-get-to-business side of the life. Here in *The Team Room*, it skewed toward more of the breaking-in phase. A young team also worked well to express my unending admiration for the apprenticeship of excellence that is the American special operations community. From one era to the next, this apprenticeship not only continues, but continues to raise the bar.

I must specifically thank all those who helped bring my second publication into existence. Lifetime comrades, family, and friends again returned as beta readers. I'm extremely lucky to have these people in my life. They are a patient lot to put up with the drafts that I send their way, and their feedback is invaluable. I was also lucky to have industry mentors return for this publication: Kathryn Johnson and Brooks Becker as editors, Rachel Lawston for cover design, and Polgarus Studios for formatting. It's a pleasure to continue soaking up lessons and insights from these amazing professionals.

During this past year of pandemic, my great love and thanks go out to Linda and E. This has been a difficult year for everyone, and a tragic year for far too many. I could not be luckier than to have been in a bubble with them, and to have their wonderful love and support. They are the absolute best.

- Bill Raskin
March, 2021

About the Author

Bill Raskin served as a career Army Special Forces officer, retiring as a lieutenant colonel with twenty years on active duty. This included wide-ranging deployments, and multiple combat tours in Afghanistan and Iraq. He led and commanded special operators at every level from small teams to command of a Special Forces battalion and battalion-level task force. He continues to consult to the national security community, and holds an MA in Security Studies and a BA in History from Georgetown University. A native of Dallas, Texas, Bill now lives in Bethesda, Maryland with his loving wife, a wonderful teen, and an awesome dog. Together they pursue many adventures. In 2019 he published *Cardiac Gap*, a debut novel. *The Team Room* is his first play.

GLOSSARY

.300 Win Mag: Refers to a practice where limited numbers of the M24 sniper rifles were up-chambered from the standard 7.62mm NATO round to a more powerful round that provided extra range.

117's: Refers to the AN/PRC-117 satellite radio.

A Team: See ODA.

A/DACG (pronounced "ay-dag"): Arrival/Departure Airfield Control Group. Essentially the airport terminal for a military base. This element coordinates the transit of personnel and equipment onto transport aircraft for stateside training or overseas deployment.

ANCOC (pronounced "ay-nock"): Advanced Non-Commissioned Officer Course.

AOR: Area of Responsibility.

B Team: The next higher level of command that oversees a Special Forces ODA. A Special Forces major commands the B Team, advised by an enlisted sergeant major. The B Team is also known by the term AOB (Advanced Operational Base) on deployment, and less commonly by the term ODB (Operational Detachment "Bravo").

BC: Battalion Commander.

BSC: Battalion support company. The headquarters administrative and logistics company for a Special Forces battalion.

Basic load: A standardized amount of ammunition, used as a point of reference for how much each soldier or unit will carry.

Bossman: Call sign for the theater airborne warning and control aircraft, through which ground teams often coordinate close air support missions.

C-141: A model of military cargo jet.

CQ: Charge of Quarters. One junior leader and an assistant assigned to man a headquarters overnight.

CASH: The actual acronym is CSH. But it's pronounced "cash." A combat support hospital.

Combatives pit: An outdoor training site used for unarmed combat training. The ground is lined with several inches of sawdust to lessen the chance of injury during falls and throws.

CONEX: Generic term for a modular storage unit, in this case an ISU-90 (see ISU-90 definition, below).

CSM: Command Sergeant Major. The senior enlisted leader in a battalion level or higher Army unit.

Dai Uy (pronounced "die-wee"): Vietnamese term for "captain." A legacy from the American intervention in Vietnam.

DMV: Desert mobility vehicle (usually pronounced "dumvee"). A 1990s-era modification to the Army standard Humvee. It included upgraded suspension, improved seats and restraint system, and other modifications.

Down Range: Literal meaning is the impact area on a firing range. The figurative meaning is to deploy overseas into a combat zone or hazardous duty environment.

E-5: The enlisted pay grade for a newly promoted sergeant, or buck sergeant. Enlisted grades run from E-1 for a private through E-9 for a sergeant major/command sergeant major.

ECAS: Emergency close air support.

GP Medium: A sixteen foot by thirty-two foot walled tent, used for base camp operations.

Group: Short for the Special Forces Group headquarters.

Half brakes: A compromise landing style in free-fall parachuting. Normally, a jumper will apply full brakes at the optimal point several feet above the ground. This will cause the chute to flare, and the jumper sinks down the final few feet to a standing landing. If anything compromises the jumper's ability to judge distance during landing (such as at night), the jumper will only apply half brakes in order to slow down, but then make a rolling parachute landing fall.

ISB: Intermediate staging base.

ISU-90: A ruggedized and standardized storage container, designed for transport on military cargo aircraft.

JTAC: Joint Terminal Attack Controller. Certification for a ground combat team member to control Air Force close air support missions and other offensive air operations.

Kit: A generic term for field tactical gear.

Klick: Slang for kilometer.

M-5 Bag: A standard issue field medical bag.

M24: Standard issue sniper rifle.

MH-47: A special operations variant of the Army's CH-47 cargo helicopter. Its twin rotors and carrying capacity are well suited to the longer travel distances and higher operational altitudes required in Afghanistan.

MRE: Meal, ready to eat. A standard field ration.

Mark-19: A model of automatic grenade launcher, usually vehicle mounted.

Med shed: Nickname for a battalion level or higher medical detachment.

Muj (pronounced "mooj"): Nickname for the US-backed Mujahideen (guerilla) fighters, during the Soviet intervention in the country.

N+2, N+4, etc: Refers to the N-hour sequence, where N stands for the official time of notification. All subsequent times refer to the number of hours following notification.

NCO: Non-Commissioned Officer. An umbrella term for all enlisted soldiers who have risen into the leadership ranks of sergeant through command sergeant major. They form the backbone of the US Army.

ODA: Operational Detachment Alpha. The central maneuver unit of Army Special Forces. Also known as A Teams. At full strength, they organize into a twelve-soldier unit.

Old man: Slang reference to a unit's commander.

Orbit: Refers to a close air support aircraft, which is orbiting on standby for a requested mission.

Pilot team: An advanced team sent into an operational theater, to make initial coordination and set the stage for larger-scale operations to follow.

PT: Physical Training. A unit's fitness program.

Q Course: The Special Forces Qualification Course.

Range book: A binder containing all of the operating procedures and policies for a given training area or firing range.

Red lens: Refers to a red lens flashlight. Soldiers use these at night so as not to ruin their adaptation to night vision.

S-2: The intelligence section for a unit staff.

Sabot rounds: A common colloquialism for harsh talk. It refers specifically to a tank main gun round that travels at ultra-high speeds.

SF: Special Forces.

Sensitive items: High value items - such as weapons, radios, and night vision equipment - which require regular accountability by serial number.

SIGDET: The signals detachment for a Special Forces Group. Responsible for base station communications out to deployed teams.

SOFLAM: Special Operations Forces Laser Acquisition Marker. A portable, tripod-mounted laser designator that teams use to guide smart bombs for precision targeting.

SOP: Standard Operating Procedure.

Spur: A small ridge line, usually an offshoot from a primary ridge line.

Tab. In a Special Forces unit, it generally refers to the Special Forces tab, which is awarded only to individuals who graduate the Qualification Course. In other combat arms units, it could also commonly refer to a Ranger tab. It may less commonly refer to the Sapper tab, or other skills or unit identifiers.

Thermals: Thermal sites, used on various weapons systems.

Top: Nickname in conventional companies sometimes given to the First Sergeant, or "top" sergeant. It is not commonly used on Special Forces teams, but was used on the first team that the author commanded.

Turn and burn: A free-fall parachuting technique to dump air from the canopy to descend faster. Colloquially means to move quickly.

Warning order: The first official order in a series of mission updates. It's designed to give subordinate units sufficient information to begin generic preparations, while commanders and staff continue to refine the operational specifics.

Wave off: The final action in military free fall before pulling the rip cord. A warning to other jumpers above or near you that you are about to activate your parachute.